Where's the Glitch?

Where's the Glitch?

How to Use Running Records with Older Readers, Grades 5–8

Mary Shea

HEINEMANN
Portsmouth, NH

Heinemann

361 Hanover Street
Portsmouth, NH 03801–3912
www.heinemann.com

Offices and agents throughout the world

The author and publisher wish to thank those who have generously given permission to reprint borrowed material:

Excerpts from "Lighting Made Easy" by Rayvon Fouché from FOOTSTEPS' January/February 2005 issue: *Ingenious Inventors*. Copyright © 2005, Carus Publishing Company, published by Cobblestone Publishing, 30 Grove Street, Suite C, Peterborough, NH 03458. All Rights Reserved. Used by permission of the publisher.

Acknowledgments for borrowed material continue on p. xviii.

Library of Congress Cataloging-in-Publication Data
Shea, Mary (Mary E.)
   Where's the glitch? : how to use running records with older readers, grades 5–8 / Mary Shea.
       p.   cm.
   Includes bibliographical references and index.
   ISBN 0-325-00849-3 (alk. paper)
   1. Reading (Middle school)—Evaluation.   2. Observation (Educational method).
I. Title.

LB1632.S437 2006
428.4071'2—dc22   2006007446

Editor: *Lois Bridges*
Production: *Vicki Kasabian*
Cover design: *Night & Day Design*
Typesetter: *Kim Arney*
Manufacturing: *Louise Richardson*

Printed in the United States of America on acid-free paper
12   RRD   4 5

*This book is dedicated to Brian and Andrew
and, in loving memory, to Don*

Contents

Acknowledgments

I t seems that so many people and experiences have had an influence on my professional life and work. Some influences are readily apparent and some go so deep that they seem to have always been a part of my core. As I try to tease these out, I wish to express gratitude to the following people from my past and present.

As I reflect on the philosophy that shapes my teaching, I know that the foundation of my belief goes back to my sixth-grade teacher, Miss Kaplan. When my family moved across town that year, I was enrolled in the neighborhood public school because a nearby private school was overcrowded. Miss Kaplan's class at Liberty Street School was a break in the traditional model I experienced before and after being there. Miss Kaplan's class was a wonderland for me. We sat at desks that could be moved; they weren't bolted to the floor in orderly rows. We arranged them in working groups that always changed. I remember being on the committee for the photosynthesis bulletin board. We were in charge! We even got to paint our leafy model in the coatroom. I never forgot photosynthesis. Miss Kaplan read to us all the time and we loved it. She read *Silver Chief: Dog of the North, George Washington Carver,* and many other books. We even wrote a script and performed a play about George Washington Carver. I was George's mother. After all these years, I vividly remember so many details about that class. Miss Kaplan made learning exciting.

I also especially remember Miss Kaplan's kindness when learning didn't come easily. That year I couldn't figure out quotation marks. She understood how frustrated I was each time I completed a paper only to find out that I had quotation marks and commas in all the wrong places. I just couldn't get it right! Miss Kaplan recognized that I was trying and let me know it. And she didn't let me continue to flounder.

She gave up part of her lunch time to tutor me. I'd walk back to school after lunch and go right into the building instead of to the playground. I suspect that Miss Kaplan presented the concept to me in a different way. In no time at all, she straightened the confusion that had reigned. I was so relieved when I understood where all the punctuation went and why; I was grateful for the support that I couldn't have fully appreciated at the time. But I do now. I remember what it felt like to not "get it." I remember what it felt like when someone helped you figure it out. Knowing Miss Kaplan made me want to be a teacher—a teacher just like her.

Students in my class have always made me understand teaching and learning in a new light. I read once that a child is someone who passes through your life and disappears into an adult. I don't believe that. Every child who has been in my life is indelibly marked in my psyche. I see the child in the faces of adults who were my students. The challenge of their unique needs and interests strengthened my skills; it formed my resolve to work harder, to learn more—to be a Miss Kaplan. What I know from study has been honed by living it out with real students in lively classrooms. My current students are older, but they too provide challenges and deep questions to explore together; they remind me that my learning never stops.

I'm fortunate to have close friends, like Ardith Cole and Elaine Garan, who nudge my thinking by gently sprinkling their seeds of wisdom into our conversations. They are mind *movers* and *groovers*; they never let grass grow under a friend's feet.

I want to acknowledge Lois Bridges at Heinemann, who, like Miss Kaplan, recognized when I needed feedback and support. Lois read drafts of chapters and responded promptly to let me know when I was on target, offtrack, or going overboard. Her mentoring manner is purely Kaplan-like in my mind! Lois' feedback is genuine and a model for sensitive delivery. She steadily encourages while guiding from the side.

I am also very grateful for each Heinemann editor along the way to publication, especially Amy Rowe and Vicki Kasabian. Their dedication to excellence is astounding and so greatly appreciated. They make me think of Cinderella's friends who scurried around to design her dress for the ball. Heinemann editors dress up my work in a way I never could. And they're always so nice while they're doing it.

I am grateful to the students and teachers who contributed to this project. They were enthusiastic about creating the examples sprinkled throughout this text. With a generous spirit, they worked with me to produce samples that would clarify the process and help teachers help students.

Lastly, but never least, I must acknowledge immediate family members who lovingly forgive my forgetfulness when I'm engrossed in a project—like my dear mother-in-law, Bernice Shea, whose card for her eighty-ninth birthday was a tad late this year. I say to them as my granddaughter, Emma, says, "I love you all the time"—even when I'm distracted.

Introduction
Running Records with Older Readers?

A running record is a method for establishing a student's "competence at a given moment in time with a specific level and type of book" (Shea 2000, 10). Running records are regularly used to track the rapidly changing development of emergent readers. "It is the most efficient, quick way of gathering reliable data that is customized to the learner" (Shea 2000, 5). Clay's protocol focuses on word reading and states that running records provide "an assessment of [students'] text reading" (2000, 3). In *Taking Running Records* (2000), I outline a procedure for doing *complete* running records with younger readers—one that includes data on reading and comprehension. This text describes a method for taking complete running records with older readers that also includes measures of text reading and comprehension. This method can be easily woven into the fabric of day-to-day teaching, assessing, and planning for instruction in middle school classrooms.

Running record data can be gathered on the spot, in the classroom, and without prepackaged materials. This makes running records superior to informal reading inventories (IRIs)—assessment packages that include short graded passages with prepared questions. Widely used IRIs have notable limitations.

Students quickly become test savvy with IRIs. This usually happens after they overhear others read passages or after they've reread several levels of passages in subsequent testing sessions. In addition, IRI passages may or may not simulate what students are expected to read every day. And, after all, we need to know how to help students read the texts we're using.

Running records have immediate relevancy; they provide timely instructional information because they're based on texts we're using in the classroom. Clay states that "having taken the record, teachers can review what happened immediately, leading to a teaching decision on the spot, or at a later time as they plan for next lessons" (2000, 4).

Based on the reliable information that records provide, we can make appropriate adjustments in the type and level of books we use with students across reading experiences. As a method of dynamic assessment, running records focus our attention on "both what the students can do individually and their potential growth as indicated by the interaction" (Dixon-Kraus 1996, 152). The data also allow immediate investigation of suspected *glitches* (problems) in a learner's road to literacy and provide specific information on the student's level of competency with texts he's expected to read. Records provide such data as well as an indication of students' mediated reading levels or "the highest level students can achieve [success with] given adult support. These levels are higher than the students' instructional reading levels and are more analogous to Vygotsky's concept of *emerging development*" (Dixon-Kraus 1996, 153). Finally, we need to find glitches that stop older readers in their tracks, derailing comprehension, engagement, and, often, cooperative participation in classroom activities. And we need to do this efficiently, in a way that doesn't bring undue attention to the adolescent reader, and in a format that's user-friendly for the content area teacher.

Like any new skill, developing the sensitive ear that hears even the slightest reading clunk seems daunting. It's one more expectation that makes our mountain of responsibility very steep. After all, don't we have enough content to teach? Middle and high school students are supposed to already be able to read. But what about those who can't read well—or well enough to successfully learn course content?

When students struggle as readers, our content knowledge and expert lesson planning won't change that condition. Learning content becomes difficult for those who are left to devise their own reading survival strategies or for those who resort to avoidance behaviors. We wonder who's responsible for repairing literacy breakdowns.

Responsibility for intervention is usually determined by the nature and severity of the problem. Literacy specialists work directly with *remedial* (at-risk) readers and provide consultant help to support and scaffold classroom teachers who are working with readers' *corrective* (less severe) problems. At the intermediate level, literacy specialists "work with content teachers to assist them in building a better understanding of the relevance of reading to their discipline, how to use their textbook effectively, and how to implement effective literacy strategies" (IRA Board of Directors 2000, 117). But where and when do intermediate teachers who are content specialists learn about assessing students' literacy skills?

Teacher certification programs at the adolescent level have begun to require literacy courses (NYSED 2004). I regularly work with secondary-level teacher candidates in these courses and sometimes have to overcome their modicum of reluctance and successfully convince them that the information outlined for the course will be relevant. Once we've begun to explore course topics, secondary-level teacher candidates are persuaded that a repertoire of effective methods for teaching literacy skills (e.g., vocabulary and comprehension) will increase students' learning of their subject content. But convincing them that they need to examine glitches in students' use of literacy skills to acquire that content is tougher. Some still regard that as the reading teacher's domain. Until they work on their running record assignment, these preservice teachers question the relevance of such an assessment measure for them. Once they've fully engaged in the experience, however, teachers accept the premise that no other assessment tool gives as much reliable, meaningful information on a student's current reading level. The key word here is *reading*. What reading entails will be discussed in Chapter 2.

Although they're sold on the idea, middle school teachers point out that, unlike their primary counterparts, they work with a greater number of students each day. This factor—numbers of students—has led middle school teachers I work with to express the following stipulation. If they were going to use running records to better understand students' literacy levels and needs with regard to the content they teach, any method for taking the records would have to consider the variables in their situation.

This text provides a *modified* process for recording students' oral reading performances that adjusts to the constraints of intermediate classrooms without compromising essential data collection. These modified running records (MRRs) efficiently assess the essential components of text processing (word-reading accuracy) and meaning processing (comprehension).

1

They Really Want to Learn

Literacy in Every Classroom

By the time students enter middle school—and certainly by high school—they're expected to have acquired basic reading skills and to be able to apply them as they read to learn curricular content. Yet those of us who have taught or are teaching at these levels know that's not always the case. Consequently, there's a great deal of content that must be read by readers who simply can't do it. These students struggle with text; there are glitches in their reading. They have trouble with word recognition or comprehension, or both. The frustration these students experience is matched by our own. Frustrated teachers realize that, although college courses prepared them to teach their content, they offered limited information on how to teach literacy skills essential for learning that content or how to figure out the sources of glitches in students' reading.

As students move into middle school, the amount of print they're expected to *process* (read and understand) with and without assistance increases steadily. Much of this is informational text. Ever mindful of local mandates and state learning standards, we systematically teach forward, attempting to *cover the curriculum* while ensuring that meaningful learning occurs. We're well prepared to teach our content and conscientious about meeting expectations. When individual students derail the learning train, putting it offtrack and off schedule, we feel confused. We wonder who's at fault. We blame students for not doing the reading and not being motivated. We blame parents for not overseeing students' studying. We blame previous teachers for passing students on when they couldn't read! It isn't our job to teach them to read. Or is it?

Decades ago, Daniel Fader (1976) proposed that we're all teachers of English, simply implying that teachers must consider the literacy skills necessary for success with the content of their courses. Language is the medium for thinking and learning (Vygotsky 1978), and students who lack the literacy skills required for processing text and expressing their understanding cannot easily transact with information communicated by authors. Goodman explains that "Language enables us to share our experiences, learn from each other, [and] plan together, and greatly enhances our intellect by linking our minds with others of our kind" (1986, 11). Regardless of seemingly logical connections between students' literacy levels and their content learning, we've questioned the veracity of Fader's claim. We've felt bushwhacked by it! No one in teacher preparation programs said we'd have to teach reading and writing too.

Many programs preparing content area teachers include content-specific methods courses, but few, if any, in teaching literacy. Only recently have some state certification offices changed regulations to require literacy methods courses (NYSED, 2004). These new regulations reflect basic principles of teaching and learning.

We all want to teach well. We're enthusiastic about our subjects. We work hard; we're prepared. We plan well. We want our students to participate, to learn, and to demonstrate their knowing in the classroom, outside of school, and on mandated assessments. But when our well-laid plans go astray for certain students, we sometimes feel ill equipped to accurately identify the source of their problems—a preliminary step in solving them.

Learning Gone Astray

Humans are programmed to learn; it's driven by our capacity to think. Our learning is continuous from the first breath we take in this world. In fact, "the thrust to learn is so natural that being deprived of the opportunity to learn is aversive . . . Inability to learn is suffocating" (Smith 1985, 89–90). But, we ask, what about those students who convincingly portray themselves as uninterested in learning?

I can't remember where I first heard the adage "Students would rather appear unwilling than unable." The truth of its message was evidenced daily in my experiences as a reading teacher. Self-defense is instinctive and the behavior described in the adage smacks of saving face.

Older troubled readers, such as those portrayed in Margaret Phinney's characterizations, often disengage (academically) when the going gets tough unless they're offered *discrete* support (Phinney 1988). These readers bear scars from previous encounters when they literally battled on their own with text. Others may have noted they were maimed but compassionately offered sympathy in place of rehabilitation that would make them whole—in their own way. These students, just as anyone else, want to learn; they want to do well and be recognized as successful. They'll find venues to accomplish those ends. It's our (parents', teachers', and community members') challenge to make sure that school is one of the venues where they find success—where they can act *willing* because we've taught in ways that make them *able*. When school success is unattainable, students seek success elsewhere and devise ways to save face in the classroom.

Flight or Fight

Cannon's (1939) research on stress concluded typical short-term responses to stress that are basic to survival. Under real or perceived stress, humans choose to react with *flight or fight* behaviors. In the midst of the situation it's often difficult to read between the lines of students' behaviors to understand what is truly being iterated, especially with the pressure of keeping the lesson on track and getting through the curriculum.

In the examples that follow, one might assume that Danny and Samantha are choosing a flight response characterized by their withdrawn and indifferent stance while Mark has selected a fight response as characterized by his belligerent tone. However well intended and sensitively delivered, our actions to change such negative student behaviors without addressing the motivation for them simply repress the behavior without eliminating the cause. But, even before we can address the cause, we must treat the calluses from multiple stress responses.

Flight

Picture this scene: After a thoughtful and thorough introduction to a chapter in their social studies text, Tom Redding asks students to silently read a few pages and respond by writing an entry in their journal. He asks them to briefly summarize key ideas and include personal reactions. This reflection will prepare readers for a whole-group discussion of the issues presented by the author. Danny, articulate on topics for which he has prior knowledge, attempts to rewrite the first sentence in each subtopic to create an acceptable summary. Samantha, who often appears quietly inattentive, has very little recorded in her journal. When circulating to monitor students' progress, Tom stops to support both of these students.

However, his attempts to scaffold Danny and Samantha seem to be met with an air of indifference.

Tom is frustrated by their usual lack of responsiveness to his sensitive, guided questioning. Although he's struggling to disregard the majority opinion, Tom begins to consider what he's heard colleagues say in the faculty room. "Danny and Samantha are unmotivated; they're lazy and just don't care if they fail." While these students are passive, Tom knows he has others who tend to erupt when approached with support in class.

Fight

As he moves on, Tom notices that Mark has the text open but doesn't appear to be reading, and nothing is recorded in his journal. Tom has experienced Mark's outbursts and carefully plans his approach. He acts as if he assumes Mark has read the pages and asks Mark if he has any questions about the reading. Mark says, "Nah." Tom tries again, asking Mark what he thought about this or that point the author made. Mark shrugs with body language that says, "No comment." Tom attempts to break down the response task to help Mark get started. He points to the first segment and asks Mark to retell that part with a gist statement, explaining that this will help him get started on a summary. Mark just stares ahead while slumping in his chair. Tom then offers to read aloud the first paragraph and allow Mark to construct a gist sentence after listening. Mark jerks up straight and sneers, "You don't hav' ta read it to me, cuz I already read it myself. But I ain't writin' no summary. This stuff is borin'."

It's About Dignity

Although their behaviors differ somewhat, Danny's, Samantha's, and Mark's reactions have more to do with protecting their dignity than with challenging Tom or simply being uncooperative. Danny's, Samantha's, and Mark's view of the interaction, understood at a conscious and subconscious level, is followed by a basic physiological response. They perceive an immediate need to save face in a stressful situation. Sometimes it's hard to identify face-saving flight or fight responses in struggling readers. Have you had situations similar to these in your classroom?

- Jay rushes through text when he reads aloud, omitting many periods and most commas. The result is a confusing mass of phrases. When asked to adjust his reading pace, he gets agitated and refuses to continue.

- After assigning independent work, you notice that Lynn is busy rearranging her notebook but hasn't started the task. When asked if she needs help, she softly says while tossing her hair, "No, but can I go to the lavatory?"
- Tara seems to understand content only after it's thoroughly discussed in class. However, she rarely participates in these discussions. She stares into her desk as if she can see through it to the floor and, when called on, quickly reiterates what someone else has said.

Having the teacher spend an inordinate amount of time asking questions and reexplaining directions while others work makes struggling readers like these extremely uncomfortable, like a deer in headlights. This becomes disconcerting, especially in front of adolescent peers.

Heavy Baggage to Unload

When working with older at-risk readers, I quickly discovered that I had to first successfully unload all the baggage weighing them down, hopefully without exploding any land mines. This baggage is constructed from all the hurt, humiliation, and failure they endured as they unsuccessfully navigated instructional terrain in schools. It has to be unloaded before students and I can work together without encumbrances. Although the removal is a delicate and risky task, it has to be accomplished before anything else will work. Identifying baggage isn't always easy, either; it doesn't come with IDs, and students aren't always aware they own it. I discover successful methods for seeking and disarming baggage through trial and error, with almost Edison-like stubbornness. Every humbling flop teaches me an important lesson, and most of the time, what works is highly individualized.

I try to remember that students' negative reactions are typically motivated by their desire to maintain personal dignity in the face of real or perceived threats. I want the environment to emanate a genuine tone of respect for one another as learners and as people. I want it to also encourage us to seek help from one another. We all have to realize that our success—theirs and mine—depends on support from each other. No one is an island. Cooperation has to go both ways for me to teach and for them to learn course content. Along with establishing a risk-free environment and a positive tone, I have to meet students' needs with regard to a third factor that impacts their learning and literacy development. This third factor relates to the materials we use. Cole (2004) categorizes these three factors (environment, tone, and materials used) as pragmatic influences and stresses their potential for enhancing or inhibiting the learning experience.

The materials we use for learning (resources) must be appropriately matched to students' interests and needs. Resource choice is the basis for the first of seven principles that the International Reading Association has outlined in its position statement on adolescent literacy: "Adolescents deserve access to a wide variety of reading material that they can and want to read" (Moore et al. 1999, 4). When these pragmatic influences are ignored, negative baggage quickly piles up. Constantly left to sink in frustrational-level material in unsupportive settings, students either drown or survive by faking reading, learning to be helpless, or disengaging totally.

Where's the Time?

With so many students, limited time, and pressure to address standards while covering curriculum, we wonder how we'll "understand the complexities of adolescent readers, respect their differences, and respond to their characteristics" (Moore et al. 1999, 8). Perhaps less is more if less is learned well; more is not more if it's not learned at all. Perhaps less is really more than enough when we carefully examine requirements against the content of texts we use. With less to cover, there's more time to *uncover*, examining content through the lens of material that students want to and can read.

Schumm, Vaughn, and Leavell present a model, the Planning Pyramid, that helps teachers "plan for inclusionary instruction and to meet the challenge of content coverage in general education classrooms for students with a broad range of academic needs" (1994, 609). The authors describe the pyramid as a mental template for teachers' examination of text content in the light of local and state objectives. This analysis allows teachers to distinguish content that all must learn, content that most will learn when it's presented in an interesting and accessible way, and, finally, content that some students will personally choose to learn. (See Figure 1–1.)

When not overwhelmed with the avalanche of information in textbooks that are "conceptually dense, inconsiderate to the reader and uninteresting" (Schumm, Vaughn, and Leavell 1994, 608), both teachers and students can meaningfully focus on what all must learn while attending to the three pragmatic influences. There's ample time to teach well, to differentiate instructional strategies and learning tasks, to meet individual needs, to reinforce, and to assess informally when we put textbook content in its proper place in the pyramid.

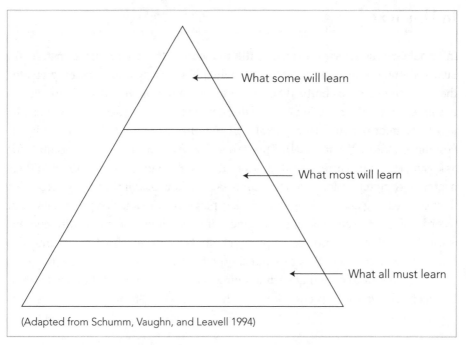

(Adapted from Schumm, Vaughn, and Leavell 1994)

figure 1–1 The Planning Pyramid: Levels of Content Learning for Unit of Study

Teaching What All Must Learn

Students don't outgrow their need for literacy instruction when they leave the primary grades. Literacy learning is never completed in those grades; it's an ongoing process. Adolescents also deserve effective instruction in, modeling of, and support with the literacy strategies they must use to understand the content of curriculum at their level (Moore et al. 1999). Students must learn to read increasingly complex texts *while* they read to learn content area concepts. To ensure success, classroom teachers teach students to read as historians, as scientists, or as mathematicians. Teaching what all must learn is most effectively accomplished when assessment is ongoing, time and space are used differently, and instruction, materials, and tasks are differentiated or matched to students' interests and needs (Tomlinson 2001; Yatvin 2004). Instruction must also consider how students perceive the methods of teaching, information, directions, and tasks presented to them. Their perceptions and understandings may not be what the teacher assumes them to be. What seems logical to the teacher may not make any sense to the student. When this is true, content and experiences become a confusing cacophony that students seek to silence.

In This Text

Informal classroom assessment lays the foundation for differentiated instruction built on attention to pragmatic factors, while efficient pyramid planning creates the time necessary for both. When teachers use multiple forms and formats for this assessment, the resulting *triangulated* data increase confidence in the reliability of the information (Eisner 1998) and the effectiveness of the differentiation (Tomlinson 2001; Yatvin 2004). This text will explain a particular procedure for assessing students' current reading level, their skills with specific texts, and their degree of comprehension through a process for taking *modified* running records of their oral reading and retelling. The book explains how to analyze the results from records, plan interventions, and implement interventions integrated with content instruction. With this process in place, students will see school as a venue for learning—a place where they can and choose to learn.

It's important to note that such learning occurs when personal understanding has been achieved. Comprehension will always be central to students' success.

2

The Bottom Line Is Comprehension

Speaking Words, Reading for Gist

Saying all the words correctly in a section of text doesn't guarantee that the speaker has constructed meaning by stringing words together and integrating them with background knowledge. I use the term *speaker* until I know that meaning was constructed. The message must be understood before the behavior can be called reading. Smith (1976) defines this understanding very simply. "Comprehension means making sense" (10), and "the process of making sense of the world by relating the unfamliar to the known is a skill" (41). Comprehension is not a quantity to be measured; it's a state of mind, of knowing, of understanding, of having questions answered. Comprehension *is* reading (Smith 1985). Fielding and Pearson (1994) define reading as a complex, recursive thinking process. Common terms found across definitions from experts include *complex, thinking, process*, and *meaning making*.

Reading comprehension involves a process and a product. We're most familiar with the concept of a product because that's what we have traditionally assessed. We attempt to measure the amount or quality of knowledge that the reader has assimilated through the reading (Johnston 1983). We check what readers remember, what they've inferred, or what they've concluded. But what part is remembered and what part is comprehended? Royer and Cunningham conclude that "comprehension processes and memory processes are inextricably intertwined"

(1978, 36) while Bower contends that "superior memory seems to be an incidental byproduct of fully understanding a text" (1978, 212).

However, remembering a component of the text is not sufficient for comprehension. Readers have comprehended text "when they have established logical connections among ideas in the text and can express them in an alternate form" (Johnston 1983, 7). Harvey and Goudvis (2000) identify these connections as text to self or students' own lives, text to other texts on the same or similar topics, and text to issues in the outside world. Too often, however, the processes that facilitate comprehension of and transaction with authors' messages have been incidentally taught and limitedly assessed.

When the product of comprehension is defective, classroom teachers sometimes lack the tools and know-how to *look under the hood* in order to examine how well the process gears are moving. Johnston suggests that glitches "can occur at the word, sentence, intersentence, or discourse level" (1983, 13) while Judith Irwin's (1991) model of comprehension points to five aspects integrating the processes and products of comprehension. Each becomes a possible area for glitches. Irwin describes five aspects that collectively constitute the very complex cognitive behavior called comprehension:

- micro (word chunking and fluency)
- macro (organizing and summarizing)
- integrative (making connections and reading between the lines—making inferences)
- elaborative (applying higher-level thinking skills and affective responses)
- metacognitive (self-monitoring and using fix-up strategies)

These aspects will be examined further in Chapter 8. Just as with any complex machine, there are many places where effective comprehension functioning can be interrupted.

Pinpointing glitches requires a thorough examination of both the processes and the products of comprehension. Completing a system check on students' reading performance requires making covert behaviors visible. Comprehension assessments that follow acts of silent reading provide data on the product of students' comprehension. But when the product is defective, these data fail to leave a trail of evidence. Students' silent, independent reading doesn't provide a window for viewing processes and identifying possible sources for problems. If we are to resolve the glitches that interrupt comprehension, we must find where the process gears are failing and realign them.

Silent and Oral Reading

In the primary grades children frequently read orally, allowing teachers to assess how well they're processing text—whether they're rolling along smoothly or experiencing bumps in the road. As readers move into fluency, reading typically turns inward and text is more often processed silently. We have efficiency indicators of silent text processing when we engage students in discussions about what they've read. However, when students' ability to demonstrate comprehension is limited, the covert act of silent reading leaves few clues that point to the source of breakdowns in understanding.

But the oral reading of text *is* a performance, and older readers, especially those who struggle with text, consider reading aloud in the presence of peers extremely stressful. Their range of competency, exacerbated by stress in public performances (e.g., round-robin reading), is revealed and sometimes becomes fodder for playground ridicule. We must find snippets of time and out-of-the-spotlight settings for older readers to demonstrate the processes they can and do use as they navigate texts they're required to read. Laura Robb (2000) explains how she accomplishes this with each of her middle school students in the first eight weeks of school. She uses classroom free-choice time to meet with each student individually for a ten- to twenty-minute session that includes an oral reading and retelling by that student. Rather than meeting with every student, I suggest setting up oral reading interactions with anyone who appears to be struggling with texts used in the classroom.

However, before we plan discreet opportunities for students' oral reading, we must reestablish their level of comfort with this performance that once was commonplace and, perhaps, comfortable for them in the primary classroom. Robb (2000) shares her purpose in requesting the student's performance much as I do when taking running records with younger children (Shea 2000). However, my wording with older readers is adjusted to their maturity level. For example, I might say:

> I'd like you to read aloud for me so I can investigate when you understand and where and why that understanding seems to break down. This will let me know what I can do to help. I'll listen as you work through the author's words and follow along with my copy. While you read, I'll be marking where your words differ from the text. I'll also ask you to tell me all about what you've read just as if I've never heard it. When we're finished, I'll share what I've recorded with you and we'll talk about it.

Establishing from the start that your purpose is to fine-tune the support you give rather than to assess for a grade activates the reader's cooperative nature. Usually, the result is a partnered approach to the task.

Reestablishing Comfort with Reading Aloud

I've always found that being straightforward works best. Students know they're having problems, and underneath the facades of indifference or bravado are cries for help. We talk about what is and isn't working. I tell them what I want to do and that I need their help. Collaboration brings many benefits.

- When students accept our expectations, they strive to reach them.
- When students understand that the assessment will make a real difference for them, they accept it as a nonthreatening tool.
- When students receive genuine, sensitively delivered feedback, they're ready to take charge of self-monitoring and self-repairing.

Openly sharing observations made during the reading of a text stimulates lively discussions, causing the reader to examine his own performance. Students soon begin to add their own insights that correct, clarify, and extend those I've shared (Shea 2000).

Once students buy in to the purpose and promise of the procedure, we have to find tolerable situations for the oral reading performances. *Round-robin reading,* an activity used in many classrooms, is not appropriate for reestablishing students' comfort level with reading aloud. Round-robin reading is a "longstanding method by which the teacher calls on students one-by-one to read orally . . . usually with little or no preparation for reading the passage" (Rasinski 2003, 17). While round-robin reading is very stressful for struggling readers, the procedure provides opportunities for them to hear the fluent reading of strong readers and a chance to assimilate text information aurally. Transforming round-robin protocol to that of *guided oral reading* maintains the benefits while nullifying stress factors. In guided oral reading, students are highly supported as they read texts—either solo or in dyads—they've practiced (Prescott-Griffin and Witherell 2004). "Reading can easily build community among students, particularly when they engage in oral reading" (Rasinski 2003, 23).

Fisher and Frey (2004) report that use of read-alouds and shared reading in secondary content area classrooms has increased in the last decade. When oral reading is used in the classroom to read and discuss texts as a whole group, individual students can be preassigned the sections (a day before) they'll read aloud. Students may choose to read solo or in tandem. Partners could even use Rasinski's *cooperative repeated reading form* (2003, 92) as they practice their reading. While students read, others listen and take notes. In a shared reading, the teacher and students read the text jointly. At other times students might be following along with a copy as the teacher or a peer reads (Fisher and Frey 2004). Such scaffolding of students' reading, grounded in Vygotskian sociocultural theory (Vygotsky 1978), extends their learning and acquisition of concepts. After the reading, the class discusses key ideas from the passage. When a class reads this way, several benefits are realized.

- Students have a chance to read and reread, practicing their part. This increases their accuracy, fluency, and word recognition.
- Students can choose to perform with the support of a partner. They can practice and perform together, making the experience less threatening.
- Listeners have a model of fluent, expressive reading as well as self-correcting and other fix-up strategies (Rasinski 2003).
- Classmates who are not reading have a chance to focus on listening and note-taking skills.
- Students for whom the text is frustrational can access the information through aural skills.
- Students recognize that reading aloud doesn't have to be intimidating.
- Students become more positively motivated to read (Herrold, Stanchfield, and Serabian 1989; Greaney and Hegarty 1987).
- Students have access to texts (and the information therein) that would be too difficult for them to read independently (Fisher and Frey 2004).
- English language learners (ELLs) are supported as they navigate texts with a bewildering array of language patterns (Fisher and Frey 2004).

Once reading aloud is again comfortably commonplace, we can look for ways to schedule times for struggling readers to read aloud for an audience of one—the teacher. This can be done with *one-minute reads* during study hall, before school, or after school. Details for successful assessment during such interactions are outlined in Chapter 3. However, success with navigating the text's words is not sufficient for, nor does it ensure, comprehension. As described previously, the reader must construct personal meaning that's logically supported by the texts; he must also be able to self-initiate a full description or *retelling* of this meaning. Chapter 5 explains how to assess students' retellings.

Retelling Versus Question-and-Answer Exchanges

Readers' self-initiated retellings accurately reveal the depth and breadth of their comprehension. "Because a retelling is usually an individual assessment, we use it when we are puzzled about how well a student comprehends a text independently . . . Our purpose is to learn what the student thinks" (Allan and Miller 2000, 171). Retelling simulates the way literate people in the world share the knowledge they've gained from texts and the interpretations they've made. Sadly, the discourse that typically follows students' reading in the classroom differs from their literate exchanges in the world. Traditional classroom question-and-answer quiz sessions (Q and As) fail to encourage or reveal students' deep understanding of texts. "Asking questions following reading has limited value in helping teachers learn about children's understanding or in developing children's ability to comprehend" (Fountas and Pinnell 1996, 79).

Teacher-posed questions often inadvertently give clues to the answers. Students begin to rely on Q and As that follow assigned reading to determine what's important to remember and the interpretations they're expected to make. They fail to build the skills necessary to initiate and participate in open academic discussions about the content of their reading. Retellings, on the other hand, allow readers to

- explicate what they conclude to be main ideas and significant details for the passage
- express personal interpretations and the evidence in the text that supports them
- describe connections they've made (text to self, text to text, text to world)
- self-monitor their comprehension as they attempt to build a full and complete retelling
- realize that reading requires an active process of constructing meaning with the text—speaking the words correctly is not enough
- develop skills in articulating their thoughts in a clear, cohesive, and concise manner (Shea 2000)

Inadequate performances may simply indicate that students are unclear about what's expected in the task or that they lack models of and experience with retelling rather than have limited comprehension (Allan and Miller 2000).

Before the teacher asks students to retell during an assessment, he should model the process and expectations repeatedly and give students ample time to practice. Using the read-aloud procedure discussed earlier, a teacher can model retelling after she or a student reads a passage aloud. After modeling the retelling protocol, the teacher can call on listeners from the audience to demonstrate retelling what they've heard. Following the criteria on the retelling form presented in Chapter 4, the class can evaluate these retellings. Have a chart of retelling criteria prominently displayed in the room. Students can use it as a cue card while they're retelling until they've internalized the criteria. Knowing the explicit expectations of the final performance and having models of what it looks like is helpful, but many readers also need to know the steps to take along the way.

Getting to Comprehension

In this chapter we've discussed what constitutes an act of reading. Summarily, reading requires comprehension that is full and complete and personally constructed. It also requires an ability to fully retell what was read in a way that clearly demonstrates such understanding. In order to identify possible inhibitors to successful reading, we need to have readers make visible the processes they use as well as the product of their engagement with texts. But before you begin to learn how to record a reader's performance, I anticipate that you want to ask a question that is frequently posed to me.

New or Known Material?

Colleagues often ask me, "Doesn't the text for a running record have to be something the student's never seen before?" This position reveals a testing stance—a stance that has a place in overall assessment. It also indicates experience with commercial informal reading inventories (IRIs) that provide leveled text segments that are new to the reader. IRIs are used to establish a reader's current level of performance in a variety of areas; they're intended to be *benchmark* measures. In other words, they act like criterion-referenced tests (CRTs), measuring the reader's performance against established levels; they do this across several tasks. These include the reader's

- level of word reading in isolation,
- accuracy of oral reading on narrative and expository text with accompanying comprehension checks,
- quality of silent reading of narrative and expository text as measured by questioning for comprehension, and
- level of listening comprehension based on questioning.

IRIs can be useful, but they have limitations.

I've found that the procedures used to administer commercial IRIs quickly decrease their reliability. When students reread passages previously scored as frustrational or overhear others reading passages, they're working from a *testwise* position. They know what's on the test; it's been rehearsed. The IRI becomes less reliable as a benchmark measure because the material was previewed. Running records (RRs) solve this dilemma.

Different Procedures for Different Purposes

When I want to have a benchmark measure, I administer what I call a *summative* running record (RR) to see what the reader can do on his own with different types and levels of text. Summative RRs measure students' overall acquired reading achievement. In this situation,

- the passage or text is new to the reader—it has not been previously heard or read;
- I consistently follow *standard* procedures for administering and scoring the running record; and
- I expect the reader to work independently.

The language arts teacher, literacy specialist, or resource teacher regularly takes benchmark RRs to determine students' overall level of performance at a given point in time. However, any teacher can take a summative RR. For example, the social studies teacher might take one to establish a student's overall instructional reading level with social studies material. But, in between benchmark points, *all* teachers need to know how students are faring with texts they're required to use day by day. *Formative* RRs provide that information on the spot, increasing the likelihood that materials, objectives, instruction, and learning activities are on target.

Day by day, on the way to benchmark RRs, I want to know how students are handling texts I'm asking them to use. This helps me plan effectively, differentiating tasks to match their needs. If students are comfortable with material, I allow more independence. If it's challenging, I provide more guidance. To determine students' level of comfort or challenge with particular texts I'm using or wish to use for instruction, I take formative RRs. I call these my *on-the-run* running records. In this situation,

- The passage can be (but doesn't have to be) a familiar one. It may have been heard, previously read, or previewed.
- A smaller section of text might be read.

- I consistently follow standard RR procedures, *but* I often use prompting when readers stumble. I do this to determine whether the prompted reader can apply strategies that she's not self-initiating. If the prompting is *heavy*—nearly giving the word—I score the prompt as an error. The reader hasn't acquired the strategy; it needs to be retaught and reinforced. If the prompt is *light*—barely suggestive—I don't score the prompt as an error. I need to encourage self-initiated use of the strategy because the reader can effectively apply it.

Formative RRs allow me to monitor a reader's pulse with any text. What I learn guides *at-the-moment* instruction and fuels plans for my next lesson.

Although both types of RRs are important, I find that content area teachers are particularly interested in formative RRs. They've recognized a timely connection with the curriculum as well as a significant, immediate impact on their teaching and students' learning.

Taking a Running Record

The next chapter describes how to set up and conduct the oral reading part of the running record. It also addresses marking codes to create a transcript of the student's reading. Examples of each marking are represented as they would appear on a running record. You can practice these markings separately using the CD that accompanies this book before recording a variety of miscues with a student reading from a text passage.

3

Taking Modified Running Records

Establishing Positive Pragmatic Influences

As previously described, pragmatic influences refer to the classroom environment, the emotional climate felt by all, and the appropriateness of the materials used. When these influences are positive, students feel comfortable and safe. They are more likely to be convinced that the running record process will help them, that its purpose is to provide us with useful information that will guide our teaching and their learning. Meeting the demands in each area of influence is a tall order, but one that can be accomplished when we understand the social, emotional, and cognitive needs of our students.

This chapter will help you get started on taking *modified* running records (MRRs) with struggling readers in your class. These are formative RRs. You can complete a modified running record on all students if you wish to assess how well each is navigating the text you're using. However, I'd suggest starting with those who seem to be having problems. Identifying the source of the difficulty and ameliorating it efficiently is critical. The quality of everyone's learning experience will be enhanced when all students feel confident and competent.

In this chapter, you'll find out how these running records are modified, how to make markings, and how to record data as students read orally. The process is nonintrusive and time efficient; it's a modification of running records used with emergent readers (Clay 2000; Shea 2000).

Modified Running Records

Traditional running records with emergent readers, typically used with selections of literature, establish a reader's independent (can read by himself), instructional (can read with help), and frustrational (too hard right now) reading levels; they also provide evidence of strategies the reader uses successfully. There's no time limit or limit on the number of words read, but I've found that the number of words usually ends up being between one hundred and two hundred. Students typically read a complete, but short, text, like a picture book. As the child reads, the teacher makes a mark for each word spoken. Words read correctly are noted by a check and each type of miscue (mistake) is recorded in a specified manner. The teacher may have a copy of the text or may just as likely follow along with the reader (Clay 2000; Shea 2000). Protocols for taking an MRR differ slightly. Modified running record protocols are a bit more time efficient. Although somewhat abbreviated, MRRs yield data as valuable as those from traditional running records—data with the potential to identify reading strengths and sources of glitches.

Overt Demonstration of Reading

Once students have become accustomed to oral reading as a classroom protocol, asking them to read aloud as we record their performance will seem less out of the ordinary. However, I still recommend that it be done discreetly. That could be while others in the class are engaged in independent work, during a study hall, or during an after-school time block. The oral reading takes one minute and the retelling a few more minutes.

One-Minute Reading Probe

Rasinski outlines an efficient procedure for assessing students' reading. It's called a "one-minute reading probe" (2003, 159). Modified running records follow this time format for the oral reading portion. Just knowing she'll have to navigate through the text for only one minute makes the task relatively painless for a struggling reader. You'll also find that more than one hundred words can be read in one minute, ensuring an adequate amount of text for reliably determining word-reading accuracy.

For the one-minute probe, select a section from a text you're using in class. It can be a section the reader hasn't come to yet. It might be a passage the student has already read silently. Or you might want to use a passage you have previously read aloud.

Getting Started

Before scheduling the MRR, make sure the environment is conducive to a productive assessment. Find a comfortable place for the interaction—one where

- the student realizes a degree of privacy,
- you're somewhat removed from the rest of the class or other students working in the room,
- noise is controlled, allowing for concentration and attentive listening, and
- there's ample room for seating, book handling, and completing the record sheet.

Reiterate the purpose of the task to the student, setting a tone for positive collaboration. Explain how his reading will help you. Tell him that you need to know what he can do well and where he needs help. More specifically, information from his MRR will guide your plans for lessons, making it easier for him and others to learn academic content. With the environment and tone set, all you'll need are the materials for the task.

From a textbook or other text being used in class, select a passage for the student to read. Have the student read from the text while you record markings on a photocopy of the passage. I like to enlarge the print size on my machine copy. It makes recording the markings easier. Explain that you'll be writing while he reads. I usually tell students:

> As you read you'll notice that I'm writing. I'm making notes on strategies you're using such as rereading and self-correcting mistakes when you notice them. I'm also recording errors you make when words are difficult or strategies aren't working for you. I'll share my notes when you're finished and we'll talk about your reading. But before we talk, I'll ask you to tell me all about what you read as if I haven't heard it. So remember to think about what you're reading as you go along.

Taping the Session

There are several good reasons for recording students' oral reading. At first, students might display a degree of apprehension about being recorded, but this reactivity factor wears off quickly once they're assured of confidentiality and the limited use of recordings. Recordings can be made to a tape, a CD, or even a video.

Video allows us to analyze students' body language cues; these are usually over-looked when we're consumed with getting the markings down. Whichever method is used, however, the reproductions

- allow us to review our markings before finalizing an evaluation
- can be used by readers to self-analyze their performance before they reread for improved word recognition and fluency
- provide evidence of students' current level of performance with texts used in class that can be shared during conferences with parents or faculty committees

I start the tape immediately and turn it off when we're finished with our conversation about the reading. That ensures that every comment, recordable behavior, or question during the interaction is captured for analysis. Listening to these later often leads to new insights.

I like to have students add additional MRRs to the same tape, which is marked with their name. We record the date and source for each reading at the beginning of the recording. At the end of the school year, students keep their own tape. It provides a sequential record of their improvement and proof positive that our collaborative hard work has paid off in noticeable reading achievement.

Activating Schemata

I introduce young readers to the book they'll be reading for the running record. I draw their attention to the title and author as well as pictures on the front and back covers. I also engage the reader in a brief *picture walk* through selected pages of the text. During the picture walk, I guide young readers in noticing illustrations and encourage them to share their predictions of the text's content. The picture walk activates the reader's schema on the text's content; the student's predictions set a purpose for reading. Similarly, I engage older readers in prereading activities that I want them to use when reading independently.

I have older readers survey the passage they'll be reading aloud. They skim to read pictures, captions, charts, marginal notations, headings, and subheadings. This activates their schema on the content covered in the passage. Sometimes, skimming builds a bit of schema where none existed beforehand. Although limited, this new schema helps the reader process information that's novel. I ask students to share their predictions or questions they expect will be answered by the author. Then I say,

> Now begin reading here [pointing to the starting place] and continue reading until I say, "Stop at the next period." I'll be saying stop after one minute.

I like to have them go to the next period to finish the thought. I've found that, in many cases, it improves the retelling. Therefore, the one-minute probe really takes one minute plus a few seconds. I add the explanation of what I'll be doing and insert a reminder about retelling at this point (as previously noted). I say:

> Try your best to read this without any help. Use the strategies you know to figure out difficult words or confusing parts. You can ask me for help, but do that only when you're really stuck.

Now the reader is ready to begin reading and I'm ready to start marking.

Marking Codes

It's important to record all markings, even those that do not count as errors. This creates a complete record of the reading event for a later review. Nonerror markings also provide qualitative insight related to the strategies students are attempting to use and should not be left unrecorded simply because they do not affect scores. I liken running records to the notations of court stenographers that allow verbatim transcripts of court proceedings to be made. To create accurate transcripts of students' oral reading performances, we need to know specific marking codes and how they're used. The marking procedure described here is adapted from Clay (1993, 2000), Goodman and Burke (1972), Johns (1997), Leslie and Caldwell (2001), and Shea (2000).

When what a reader says differs from the text, she's made an error. This difference could be due to a word substitution, an omission, an insertion, or various other types of misreading. Goodman (1976) identified reading errors as *miscues* because they indicated that the reader has missed a cue in the text that should have led to a correct decoding of the author's words. Let's consider a few general points to keep in mind as you begin to take an MRR.

There is a one-to-one match between text words and markings. Only one error can match with a word of text. For example, if a student reads *do not* for the word *don't* in the text, it counts as two errors. But only one of the errors is matched to *don't*. The word *do* is marked as a substitution for *don't*, and *not* is recorded as an insertion.

$$\frac{do \quad not}{don't} \; {}^{\wedge} = 2 \text{ errors; } 1 \text{ substitution } (do \text{ for } don't) \text{ and } 1 \text{ insertion}$$

If a student abandons a substitution and comes up with another incorrect word, record the second attempt, but score only one error for the misread text word.

infection

~~in-fec-te-us~~

infectious

When students read a word correctly and then, believing they've misread it, abandon it for a substitution, the substitution counts as an error.

✗ evidence   ✗ re-pair-a-tions

evident   reparations

Abandoning a word read correctly often indicates that the reader is not familiar with it even though he initially decoded it accurately or he doesn't understand how the word he read fits the context. The following descriptions of markings used in the MRR elaborate on these points and also provide more details on errors and nonerrors.

Words Read Correctly

You don't have to mark words read correctly on your machine copy of the text as you follow along with the reader. The absence of markings indicates that words were read correctly. However, if you notice that readers become uncomfortable each time your pen moves to record an error, make a check over all words read correctly. That way the pen is constantly moving—recording correct reading as well as miscues. This next example shows how to mark correctly read words.

✓ ✓ ✓ ✓   ✓   ✓   ✓   ✓   ✓   ✓
On the way west, wagoners crossed turbulent rivers with caution
✓   ✓
and courage.

Word Substitutions

When words are read incorrectly, record the substitution above the word in the text. Substitution miscues count as errors.

After he died, the pharaoh's body was prepared for ~~burial~~ *buried*. His
internal organs were removed and placed in stone jars.

1 error

When names or other proper nouns are misread over and over with the same substitution, they count only once as an error. These substitutions seldom interrupt meaning. However, if the reader changes the error to a different attempt on the word, that second substitution counts as an error.

The mummy of the King Khafre was buried in a tomb inside a
pyramid. The Great ~~Sphinx~~ *Spin-x* was built to guard his pyramid. In the
beginning it was beautifully painted, but over time harsh weather
damaged the Great ~~Sphinx~~ *Spin-x*. Amazingly, the Great ~~Sphinx~~ *Spink* is still
standing guard after 4000 years.

2 errors

Other substitutions count every time even though the same word is substituted because each occurrence typically interrupts meaning.

It was believed that the soul of the ~~pharaoh~~ *par-ā-oh* left this world to join the
gods. The ~~pharaoh~~ *par-ā-oh's* family brought his mummy and many treasures
to the tomb inside the pyramid. They believed the ~~pharaoh~~ *par-ā-oh* needed
these in his new life.

3 errors

Multiple Attempts on a Word

Try to record all attempts on a word. Sounding out can be recorded with lowercase letters and phonetic markings. The check following the representation of sounding out the word in the following example indicates that the segments were blended to iterate the whole word correctly.

rep-re-hen-sible ✓
─────────────────
reprehensible

Self-Corrections

When students' subsequent attempts correct a miscue, indicate that the correct word was eventually read by writing SC for *self-corrected*. Self-corrections do not count as errors.

People believed that the pharaoh's soul flew up to ~~rejoin~~ the gods.

regit...region SC

0 errors

Omission of Words

Circle words that the student missed reading. Circle omitted punctuation (e.g., commas, periods). Omitted words are counted as errors. Omitted punctuation marks are not counted as errors. However, it's important to note the reader's lack of attention to punctuation, as it could be a significant factor related to her confusion.

Throughout history robbers have broken into pyramids to steal (valuable) treasures.

1 error

Repetitions

Students make repetitions for a variety of reasons. Sometimes it's to go back and correct an error once they realize they've made it. Sometimes they repeat to get another start or more meaning to figure out a new word. In moderation, repetitions are beneficial for word accuracy and keeping meaning intact. Repetitions do not count as errors. However, if repeating becomes habitual, it can inhibit comprehension. Draw a line under the repeated word or words. Stop with an arrow at the point where the repetition started and record an R at the end of the repeat. If the word or words are repeated again, write a subscript number after the R to indicate how many more times the words were repeated. For example, write R_2.

Robbers even found secret ~~tombs~~ in a rocky place called the Valley of the Kings. Howard Carter, a British archaeologist, found the treasures of King Tutankhamen hidden in the Valley of the Kings.

0 errors

Word Insertions

Sometimes readers insert words that make sense or even improve the text. At other times they are adding words to make a miscue make sense or fit grammatically. Record the word inserted by writing it above a caret.

The tomb of King Tutankhamen had never been robbed. It

remained untouched for $_\wedge$ 3000 years. Inside, Carter found a chamber

over

with $_\wedge$ valuable ~~treasures~~. He also found the mummy of King

a   *treasure*

Tutankhamen beyond the chamber.

3 errors

Appeals for Help and Teacher-Given Words

When the reader stops dead in his tracks and indicates that he wants help (verbally or through body language), mark an A to indicate an appeal for help. First, encourage him to use the strategies he knows to figure out the word. The appeal itself doesn't constitute an error. If the reader doesn't try to figure it out himself, say the word. Mark TG (teacher-given) above the word you read for the student (A-TG). Sometimes the student doesn't request the word, but simply won't attack it, even with encouragement or prompts. At this juncture, give him the word and mark TG over it, but do not record an A (appeal for help) in this situation. Words given by the teacher are counted as errors.

Thousands of people worked on building the pyramids. First they

had to cut huge stones out of rock ~~quarries~~. Then, these stones

A-TG

were loaded on wooden ~~sledges~~ and pulled to boats.

TG

2 errors

Starting Over

Sometimes a series of errors in a section causes so much confusion that the reader can't seem to get back on track. Stop the reading and suggest a repetition to self-correct miscues and get back to meaning. Say:

Let's stop. It isn't making sense. You need to go back here and start over. Reread this part carefully so that it makes sense and then continue. I'm sure you'll correct the errors that caused the confusion and be back on track.

Point to where you want the reader to begin the repetition. Place a bracket around the section of text that will be repeated and mark SO for *start over* outside of the bracket. The SO counts as one error since the repetition was directed by you rather than self-initiated by the reader. Hopefully, the reader will self-correct most of the miscues that created the confusion, lessening the overall error count for the section.

3 errors

Pronunciation Shifts

Sometimes readers mispronounce words in a way that changes them to another word. At other times, their mispronunciation results in a nonword. Either way, it counts as an error. However, when words are misarticulated because of characteristic dialectal differences associated with regional, cultural, or personal speech patterns, they do not count as errors. In such cases the reader is reading the word correctly according to her speech pattern.

The archeologist made a ~~record~~ of all the treasures found in the tomb.   1 error

[The student said "re-'CORD," as in "write down."]

or

The archeologist made a ~~record~~ of all the treasures found in the tomb.

1 error

Reversing Word Order

Students sometimes transpose the order of words when they read. I've found this to happen when they're following a previous word pattern used by the author.

Typically, reversals do not interrupt meaning. However, an error is still recorded for each word reversed using a ⌒‿ symbol around the transposed words. Following the word-to-word matching protocol, the reader's reversal creates two substitutions.

The archeologist cautioned the team of workers at the site.

"Handle each item carefully and record its number accurately,"

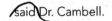 said Dr. Cambell.

2 errors

Interventions During the Running Record

When the one-minute probe is purely diagnostic—to identify what the reader can do on his own—I stick to what I've told the student. He should figure out words on his own, using the strategies he knows as he reads. Unless there's an appeal for help or the reader stalls, I don't prompt. However, there are times when I intentionally use prompts with a reader.

I might give a prompt to determine whether the student knows a particular strategy and can use it once prompted to do so even though she failed to self-initiate its use. If my prompting is exaggerated and leads the reader to finally decode the word correctly, I record the type of prompt I used and count it as an error. If my prompt was slight (e.g., a suggestion to use a particular strategy or a hint) and the reader gets the word, I don't count the prompt as an error. If the student still reads the word incorrectly after I prompt, the substitution counts as an error, but the prompt doesn't add an additional error since only one error can be scored on each word.

Prompting is a subjective decision, one based on circumstances, my knowledge of the reader, and the information I'm seeking about his competency level. Prompting allows me to consider how close the reader is to self-initiating strategies.

Codes for Teacher-Prompted Strategies	Strategies Suggested by Prompts
P-cc	Student prompted to try context clues
P-pc	Student prompted to use picture (chart, organizer, etc.) clues
P-sc	Student prompted to use sound or structure clues

Hesitations

Sometimes readers pause as they approach an unknown word. Mark any significant hesitation (three to four seconds) with an H at the point that it occurs. Hesitations do not count as errors. However, it's important to make note of them because they tend to interrupt fluency.

The mummy of the pharaoh was placed in a coffin called a

H

sarcophagus.

∧

0 errors

Figure 3–1, shown on the next page, summarizes these markings, noting which count as errors and which are nonerrors.

Although some reading inventories present two reading accuracy scores—one counting only errors that interrupt meaning and another that counts every error—all errors are tallied in this procedure. I found that using the total error count for word-accuracy scores ensures consistency across a school site and district. This issue is discussed further in Chapter 7. Individual decisions on meaningfulness of miscues can result in inflated or deflated word-reading scores when errors that didn't affect meaning are not factored in. I make sure to discuss instances where the reader's miscues did not affect her understanding of the text in summary comments that I write. Sometimes, such errors even improve the text or reflect the use of a particular strategy. For example, I might write:

> Although Jamie's word-reading score was in the instructional range, several of her errors were meaningful substitutions. When unfamiliar with a word used in the text, she was able to discern enough meaning from context to replace it with an appropriate synonym. Developing the vocabulary for a selection before reading will be important for Jamie.

Recording Data During the Reading

Figure 3–2 provides an example of markings recorded during a one-minute probe. Errors and specific nonerrors were transferred to a tally sheet for analysis and record-keeping purposes (see Figure 3–3). The marked copy of the text is attached to the tally sheet along with a retelling checklist, which is described in the next chapter. These documents are filed in the student's portfolio as evidence of developing competencies.

Miscues That Count as Errors	Nonerrors
Generally, count all substitutions as errors, even repeated substitutions for the same word each time they're used. However, see box to the right for an exception related to proper nouns.	Repetitions of substitutions for proper nouns are not scored as errors. Consistent substitutions for proper nouns count only the first time. If a different substitution is subsequently used for that proper noun, an additional error is counted. (For example, if a reader read *U.S.* for *United States* several times, it would be scored as an error only once. If the reader then read *America* for *United States*, another error would be scored.)
Omissions	Self-initiated repetitions
Insertions	Multiple incorrect attempts when figuring out a word before it's finally read correctly
Teacher-given words	Hesitations
Starting over (teacher-suggested repetition)	Dialectical differences in the articulation of a word (if pronunciation used is characteristic of student's speech pattern)
Word reversals (one error for each word reversed)	Omitted punctuation
Pronunciation shifts that change the word to another word or a nonword	Self-corrections
Prompts (count as an error based on teacher decision)	Prompts (do not count as an error based on teacher decision)

Additional Scoring Guidelines

The reader can have more errors than words on a line, but not more errors than words on a page. Whenever the error count would be higher than the number of words on a page, use the number of words on the page as the error count for that page.

    If a line of print or sentence is omitted, count each word as an error. However, it's a good idea to send the reader back to that line or sentence. Teacher-directed repeats or directions to start over (SO) count as one error but usually cause the reader to make several self-corrections. When the reader starts over, the rereading—not the first reading—is scored. If a whole page is missed because the reader turned two pages instead of one, the missed words don't count as errors. However, this would likely affect the reader's understanding. For that reason, a teacher-directed repeat (SO) is also recommended in this case.

    When a word is read as two words, it is regarded as a pronunciation error unless it changes meaning. For example, if the reader read *away with* as *a way with*, two errors would be counted. The word *a* would be an insertion and *way* would be a substitution for *away*.

figure 3–1 Summary of Running Record Markings

Frith's Fabulous Photography
By: Shannon Thomas Perich

In Frith's day, 'instant' photos meant a total of six on a good day.

In 1855, at age 34, Francis Frith ~~retired~~ [*sc* retried]. After a successful career in the grocery and printing business, he felt a (bit) [①R] restless and unsure of what challenges he should ~~pursue~~ [② follow]. He decided to travel. Between 1856 and 1860, Frith made three trips from his homeland, England, to Egypt. The first was one of photographic ~~experimentation~~ [③ experiments]. No one really knew how Egypt's weather and sun, both of which were much more intense than ~~England's~~ [④ England], would ~~affect~~ [⑤ a·flect] a photographer's ability to make ~~collodion~~ [⑥ his colo de in ⑦] negatives. Frith and a colleague discovered that with care, photographs could be made. The success of this trip led to two more photographic ~~expeditions~~ [⑧ TG R] in Egypt.

On these trips, Frith took a specially crafted wagon. All of the ~~collodion~~ [⑨ colo de in] negatives he created were on glass, which had to survive the trip to, through, and from Egypt. / On a good day, Frith could make six large negatives. Negatives were made by preparing the emulsion, pouring it onto one piece of glass, placing a glass plate in the camera, exposing the plate while the emulsion was still sticky (a real feat in Egypt's hot, dry weather), and then finally developing the image.

9 errors

figure 3–2 Sample of Markings on Section of Text

Reader ___**Bill**_____ Date _____

Recorder _____

Text read ___**Frith's Fabulous Photography**_____ Pages __**26**__

1. Introduce the selection. Skim through the section of text, inviting reactions from the student and guiding logical predictions on the text's content.
2. Ask the student to begin reading. Explain that you will ask him to stop after one minute. Also explain that you'll be making notes during the reading. You'll use the notes to start a conversation about what went well and where help is needed.
3. Record all of the reader's changes from the text and words given (miscues) along with self-corrections and repetitions on a copy of the page(s) as he reads. Shorthand and abbreviations are recommended to facilitate recording.
4. Have the *Running Record Marking Codes* handy until the coding becomes familiar. Later, the information is transferred to this sheet. Substitutions, insertions, omissions, mispronunciations, and teacher-given words are counted as errors. Self-corrections and repetitions are *not* counted as errors.

Substitutions	MA*			Insertions	M**	Omissions	M	Mispronun- ciations	M
Text/ Substitution	M	S	L-S		Y/N		Y/N		Y/N
pursue/follow	✓	✓	—	his	N	bit	N	collodian affect	Y Y
experimentation/ experiments	✓	✓	✓						
England's/ England	✓	—	✓						

*MA = miscue analysis; M = meaningful substitution, S = syntactic structure of sentence maintained, L-S = substitution has a minimal letter-sound similarity with the text word
**M = passage meaning interrupted

Teacher-given words	Self-corrections	Number of repetitions
expeditions	Text word corrected—Initial miscue retired- retried	2

5. When one minute is up, note the last word read. Other areas listed here can be completed later.

Last word read **Egypt**_____ Paragraph # **2nd**__ Number of words in text to that point __**138**__

Number of self-corrections _**1**_ Number of errors _**9**_ Number of words read correctly __**129**__

Percent of errors self-corrected _**10**_ Error Rate **1:15** Words correct per minute (WCPM) ____

Fluency Rubric Score _____ **Percent of Accuracy** __**93**_____

figure 3-3 One-Minute Probe Tally Sheet

Before reading the selection from *Dig* magazine (Figure 3–2), Bill skimmed the article. He read the captions under each picture and the author's explanation of photographic emulsions in the margin. The word *collodion* (a solution used in the manufacture of photographic film) is somewhat explained in that note. Bill also read the article's title and subtitle and generated predictions on what he expected to find out. The one-minute probe began as Bill started with the first paragraph and ended with the word *Egypt* (as marked). He read 138 words during the probe and made nine errors. I counted each number (e.g., *1855, 34*) as one word. Bill read 129 out of 138 words correctly, giving him a score of 93 percent for word-reading accuracy. But what does that tell us? To answer that, we must transfer data from the to the tally sheet and analyze them.

Immediately after the one minute of reading, I ask the reader to retell what he just read as if I haven't just heard it. I don't want him to forget or get distracted before he can share his understanding of the content. Retelling is discussed in Chapter 4. However, while we're examining the markings, let's look ahead to how data from Bill's probe were later transferred to a tally sheet for analysis.

After finishing the complete modified running record—a one-minute probe and a retelling—I briefly discuss highlights with the reader. I stick to one or two teaching points. Later, I transfer data from the marking sheet to the tally sheet. Figure 3–3 demonstrates where data from Bill's probe were placed on the tally sheet and shows the tallies for his errors and nonerrors. You'll notice one calculation, *error rate*, that hasn't been addressed. As an approximation of how frequently errors interrupted the flow of reading, this score provides a measure of fluency. Directions for calculating the error rate are included in Chapter 5. Directions for calculating the WCPM and fluency score are discussed in Chapter 6.

Conclusions

I have to share one caveat with you now that you've mastered the markings for a modified running record. They become implanted in your mind in a way that can be a bit of a nuisance. Whenever I have a copy of the text in my hands while listening to someone read it, I do a mental running record. I can't turn it off! Instead of paying attention to the message, I'm checking off meaningful substitutions, omissions, repetitions, and on and on. I'm sure that's not what some readers expect from me. That's why I never share my mental analysis of his word-reading accuracy on the gospel with my pastor.

Now you're ready to give it a try! Use the scripts and recordings found on the CD to practice miscues as students read. With continuous practice, your recognition of and ability to record readers' miscues will be refined to the point that they're automatic skills. But that's only the first step.

To complete the picture of a reader's current level of competence with a particular text, I want to know how well she understood what she decoded. Saying the words is not enough. If the reader has not understood the words and overall passage, she hasn't really read.

The next chapter discusses retelling, specifically the power of retelling as a measure of comprehension. You'll find out how to direct retellings that complete MRRs. The CD also provides models for scoring and evaluating students' retelling. Use these scripts and recordings to practice after reading Chapter 4.

Appendix 3-1: Summary of Modified Running Record

Code	Explanation	Example	Counted as Error
✓	Word read correctly	✓ ✓ ✓ ✓	NA
incorrect word / text word	Reader makes a substitution for the word in the text	commute / compute	Yes
SC	Reader self-corrects an error	~~commute~~ SC / compute	No, but number of SCs is reported.
⬭ (omitted word is written inside of the oval)	Reader omits a word	(charred)	Yes
∧	Reader inserts a word	the ∧	Yes
TG	Teacher-given word	TG / compute	Yes
A	Student asks for the word. Teacher gives the word	A–TG / fossils	Yes (1 error for the A followed by the TG)
SO	The teacher directs the student to a place where she should *start over*. It's a teacher-initiated repeat.	somewhere they] SO / sometimes it]	Yes, the SO counts as 1 error. Hopefully, it stimulates several SCs.
◄——— R	Repetition	✓✓✓✓ / ◄——— R / If the words are repeated again, write a subscript with the R (e.g., ◄——— R_3)	No
H	Hesitation	H ✓ / specifically	No
～	Reverse word order	said ～ Dad	Yes, score the reversal as 2 errors—one for each word reversed.
dialectal variation of text word	Reader's pronunciation matches a consistent personal dialectal variation	mus / must	No, not counted unless the student pronounces it conventionally in other situations.

(Adapted from Shea 2000)

Appendix 3–2: Steps for Conducting a Modified Running Record

1. Schedule a session for the MRR for a time when other students are working independently, during a study hall, or during an after-school time block.
2. Prepare the environment. It should be comfortable for the reader and recorder, relatively quiet, and allow for a degree of performance privacy.
3. Start the taping equipment. State the date and the reader's name and identify the selection.

> Today is February 12, 2005. Bill Thompson will begin reading on page 134 with the section titled "Causes of the Civil War."

4. Reiterate the purpose of the MRR and what you'll be doing while the student reads.

> Bill, I'd like you to read aloud from this book that we're using in class so I can see the strategies you use when you're figuring out new words and making sense of what you're reading. I'll use that information to plan lessons that focus on what you need to know.
>
> As you read you'll notice that I'm writing. I'm making notes on what I see. I'm watching for the strategies you're using, such as rereading and self-correcting mistakes when you notice them. I'm also recording errors you make when words are difficult or strategies aren't working for you. I'll share my notes when you're finished and we'll talk about your reading.

5. Introduce the reading selection. Ask questions to determine background knowledge. Have the student skim the selection, reading pictures, captions, charts, marginal information, headings, and subheadings. Invite the reader to share comments, predictions, and questions he expects to be answered.
6. Give directions for the task.

> Now, begin reading here [*point to the starting place*] and continue reading until I say, "Stop at the next period." I'll be saying stop after one minute. Don't be concerned about the time; I'll watch the clock and let you know when to stop. The goal is to understand what you've read rather than just get through a lot of words in the minute. So, read at a pace that makes it sound like talking and allows you to think about meaning.
>
> Try your best to read without any help. Use the strategies you know to figure out difficult words or confusing parts. You can ask me for help, but do that only when you're really stuck.
>
> When the one minute for reading is up, I'll ask you to tell me all about what you read as if I haven't heard it. So remember to think about what you're reading as you go along.

7. Allow the student to read for one minute while you record markings on a machine copy of the text.

8. Stop the student after the minute is up, allowing him to get to the next period. Compliment the student's persistence with the task. Then ask him to retell.

    Now, tell me about what you just read as if I haven't heard it before.

    If the student stops talking, ask, "Anything else?" Repeat this request, which does not give away information but lets the reader know that you're expecting to hear more about his recall, interpretations, or conclusions. Check *unassisted* in areas on the retelling checklist where the reader fully self-initiated the retell or responded to the limited probe of "Anything else?"
      When the reader has exhausted what he can retell, ask questions directed at areas of the retelling checklist that have not been commented on.

    Bill, in this section the author also told which cause he concluded to be the main cause of the Civil War. Can you tell me about that?

    If the student can respond appropriately to the question, check that area of the retelling checklist under *assisted* retell since you had to probe more specifically for the response. The student understands what he read but needs assistance in realizing or expressing his knowledge.

9. Briefly share highlights of your notes with the student. Stick to one or two teaching points. For example, a teaching point might be where context clues would have helped him identify an unknown word. Another might be about noticing the signals that an important point was coming in the paragraph. These will be strategies you'll both plan to focus on.
      Thank the student for working cooperatively with you and direct him to his next activity or class.

10. Complete the tally sheet and summaries of results, comments, and conclusions.

4

Completing the Record

Why Retelling?

My goal throughout an investigation of students' reading competency with classroom texts is to determine the meanings they've constructed and connections they've made with the content. As Allan and Miller (2000) suggest, I choose to use retelling because I want to see what readers can initially recall, infer, wonder, or conclude *without* any clues from my questions. Basically, I want to determine whether the reader has constructed meaning with this segment of text. But I also need to know if she's confident and competent in being able to thoroughly explain her thinking on her own, without prompting. I expect more than a summary that includes a gist statement (main idea) with a few significant details. A summary won't let me know how deeply the reader has engaged with the content. I want the reader to *retell*. I expect her to talk, talk, talk—talk about, through, into, and across the content of what she read.

Retelling is different from summarizing. Summaries rephrase the gist of the text; they might include a modicum of inference with one's determination of a main idea. On the other hand, retellings are supersized, *summary-plus* responses. Students' retellings reveal the range, depth, and personal nature of their understanding; retellings resemble in-the-world literate interactions.

The Retelling Performance

Retelling and answering direct questions call for very different *production demands.* Retellings require readers to elaborate on what they considered important. This means that the reader *maintains the floor* as the speaker with self-initiated telling. There's a steady stream of talk—a monologue that clearly expresses what the text was about as well as connections, inferences, and conclusions the reader has made. When the retelling is finished, the listener can begin to respond or pose questions. Walker (2004) suggests that students' talking provides a window on their developing expressive language skills as well as their thinking. "Retellings can also indicate students' ability to organize and elaborate verbal responses" (24). These verbal elaborations improve the comprehension of less fluent readers (Koskinen et al. 1988). In contrast, direct questions call for circumscribed answers that match students' reasoning processes to the types of questions posed. Direct questions are typically structured to confine students' replies (Tierney, Readence, and Dishner 1995).

With a direction like "Start from the beginning and tell me all about what you read as if I haven't heard it before," the ball is in the reader's court. I prompt with a simple probe, "Anything else?" until the reader indicates, "That's all." At that point, I begin to engage the reader in conversation about the text by posing comments or questions.

Routman (2003) suggests using general questions designed to probe for more talk from the reader when there appears to be a glitch in understanding—a significant missing link. Figure 4–1 provides a list of questions that I might use with expository and narrative texts. To explore specific areas of the retelling checklist that the reader hasn't addressed, I form questions for her that are intended to elicit more retelling. I always customize my questions so they're appropriate for the selection just read, and I use them selectively, as needed.

When the reader answers a question appropriately, I score this area as an assisted retelling. Of course, if a particular area on the checklist (e.g., interpreted visuals) doesn't apply to the situation, I record NA on the form in that block.

I use retelling to move my assessment beyond the accuracy of word reading to an assessment of the reader's meaning making—with any content. Tierney, Readence, and Dishner state, "Retelling can be used across the curriculum with a variety of grade levels" (1995, 517). Retelling initiates a consolidation of the reading; it completes the MRR.

Possible questions for probing students' understanding of expository text (based on the Retelling with Expository Text Checklist)

1. What's the gist of what you read—what's this section mostly about?
2. Can you identify terms the author used that are related to the topic?
3. Can you explain the structure used in this section to organize the content?
4. What ideas do you have about what you learned?
5. What did you learn from the charts (or other visuals)?
6. Did this remind you of something else you learned on this topic?
7. Did the author present the information clearly?
8. Was it interesting? Why?

Possible questions for probing students' understanding of narrative text (based on Retelling with a Narrative Text or Poem Checklist)

1. What's the gist of what you read—what's this section mostly about?
2. Where is this story taking place?
3. Who are the characters mentioned here?
4. What's the problem?
5. What's the main character like?
6. What new words or expressions have you learned?
7. Did the author's style hold your attention?
8. Do you want to read more? Why?
9. Did you make any connections with the story or characters?

figure 4–1 Questions for Assisting a Retelling

Retelling Completes the Record

The oral reading sample provides indications of the reader's ability to decode words, read smoothly, monitor her performance, and apply fix-up strategies. Although these behaviors are important, they don't guarantee comprehension. And without understanding, *reading* just didn't happed. It was only *word speaking*—gibberish in the mind of the reader! To complete the MRR assessment, I have to measure the depth of the reader's comprehension.

Traditional oral reading assessments (informal reading inventories, or IRIs) use prepared questions to check the reader's comprehension of a passage. The questions vary in type but are often leading, they have obvious answers and sometimes can be answered using only background knowledge. I find these questions to be surface skimmers; they never seem to reach any depth or evoke personal interpretations. They create *school readers* who expect the Q-and-A format after any reading event. Students begin to wait for the Q and A instead of sharing reactions. Correctly answering the teacher's questions provides readers with a sense of success; it's also easier than supporting personal viewpoints in a discussion. Fountas and Pinnell (1996) state that asking students comprehension questions after they've read has limited value in helping us determine their understanding. The question format probably stunts students' development of self-directed meaning making and comprehension self-monitoring. When this happens, we begin to think students can't or aren't ready to engage in genuine discourse, so we ask more questions—and the prophecy is fulfilled. But the real world expects a different response after reading.

When I'm finished reading a book I've enjoyed, my reading friends and I want to talk about it. We're eager to share impressions and interpretations. We talk, agree, debate, and go back to the text for evidence to support our stance. We sometimes ask questions, but only to probe each other's comments. When students have finished reading, I want them to talk about what they've read in a genuine way, just as people do outside of school. *Retelling* allows this. It also completes the MRR, providing an indicator of the reader's level of comprehension.

Guiding the Retelling

What Is a Retelling?

Retelling is just what the term implies. The process requires the reader to tell about what he just read as if the listener hasn't heard it before. But, as already stated, retellings don't simply encapsulate the text's central theme; they're much more than that. A full and complete retelling includes a summarization of key points, a presentation of interpretations, a sharing of personal connections, and a description of the conclusions the reader has drawn. Each aspect of the full and complete retelling reflects the depth of the reader's meaning making with the text.

Getting Ready to Retell

I find that it helps to remind readers that I'll be asking them to retell what they've read in their own words, even when I'm not doing an MRR. Being prepared to discuss what they're thinking becomes a habit of mind; it's what good readers are ready to do.

I want my students to be comfortable with the procedures for retelling. In *Taking Running Records*, I suggest giving explicit instruction, modeling, and allowing plenty of practice in the retelling protocol before using this procedure for assessment (Shea 2000). I model, model, model the act of retelling after teacher and peer read-alouds. Lots of supportive practices, genuine feedback, and group analyses of exemplary retellings clarify expectations for the task. I also suggest hanging a cue chart in the room; this guides students through the retelling steps. (See Figure 4–2.)

Initiating retelling as a follow-up to reading takes patience and persistence. Whenever it seems like a struggle, I talk myself through the bumpiness; I encourage myself not give up on readers and go back to Q and As.

Making students comfortable with the retelling technique also improves the quality of assessment data I gather on their comprehension as well as their self-monitoring for learning. Building comfort with retelling is time well spent; the dividends are huge. Through retelling, students

- become more engaged with the text, discerning what they'll tell
- demonstrate recall of key concepts presented in the text
- weave personal interpretations and connections into their meaning making
- learn to self-assess where their comprehension is full and where it's lacking
- begin to understand that reading requires continuous critical thinking—a mental conversation with the author
- develop more sophisticated language structures for conversing about what they've read
- gain confidence in expressing their ideas

Effectively communicating the rationale for retelling ensures that students will begin to recognize the benefits this skill holds for them. It's also important to always let students know up front that you'll expect them to retell what they've read to show their understanding.

Starting to Retell: What Should Readers Tell in a Retelling?

I start slowly, with patience and faith that students can do this and do it well. I try to remember that Rome wasn't built in a day. That means I can't expect a quality retelling after the first introduction to the process. Students need ample time to practice and specific feedback on their performance after the retelling steps have been clearly explained and modeled.

Introduction, Summary, and CIREC—Steps for Retelling

Introduction:

1. Begin with an introduction.

   _____ (name of the text read) by _____ (author) is a/an _____ (genre, e.g., narrative, informational piece) that's all about _____ (topic).

Summary (that integrates key or interesting vocabulary in the writing):

2. If the selection is a narrative, focus on the story elements that were included in the sample of text you read. Add details that seem to be important.

   _____ by _____ is a narrative that's all about _____. In the section I read, _____, the main character, . . .

3. If the selection was informational, consider the structure of the section you read as well as important terms found in the writing. Were a cause and an effect discussed? Were two or more things compared? Was a description presented? Was there a sequence outlined? Did the author present an opinion and give a rationale for it? Frame your retelling of key concepts in a way that follows the structure in the text. For example, if the section you read compared the military strength of the Union and Confederate armies at the start of the Civil War, you'd use a compare-and-contrast format to shape your retelling.

   _____ by _____ is an informational book about the Civil War. I read a section that compared the strength of the Union and Confederate armies at the beginning of the war. There were several similarities in the Union and Confederate armies. Both had . . . However, there were important differences too. The Union army . . . The Confederate army . . .

Connections, Interpretations, Reactions, Evaluation, and Conclusions (CIREC):

4. Don't forget to make connections to experiences or other books, add personal interpretations, share reactions, describe your evaluations of the writing, and explain your conclusions. You can use the following to guide your retelling.

   C: Tell how this compares with what you knew before.
   I: Share your thinking.
   R: Explain your reactions. How did it make you feel?
   E: Tell what was exciting or interesting.
   E: Talk about the writer's style.
   C: What conclusions have you made so far?

   I think the armies were matched in number at the beginning of the war. (I) I didn't realize how young many soldiers were. (R) The writer added this to grab our attention and make us think, "These soldiers were close to my age!" (E) It seems that many weren't well prepared or well equipped. (I) They were expecting a big adventure and found out how horrible war really was. (I) Our textbook didn't bring this out, but the video we watched yesterday seemed to. (C) I think poor training and poor equipment could be a big reason that the Civil War had so many deaths. (C)

figure 4–2 Guidelines for a Retelling

I teach the components of quality retellings for different genres by going over categories of information and ideas identified on checklists I use for assessing retelling performance (see Figures 4–3 and 4–4). I emphasize that although good retellings are customized to the content of what was read, each includes categories of information and opinion. When reading a narrative passage, students should consider

- story grammar revealed in the reading
- the relationship of this section to the whole
- details related to any unfolding event
- their analysis of the event
- character traits they've inferred
- confirmation of their predictions or predictions for the next part
- connections they've made
- their evaluations on the writing
- conclusions they've reached

When reading an informational passage, students should consider

- the structure of the writing—whether the writing describes, explains a cause-and-effect relationship, compares one or more things, presents a proposition with support, or outlines a sequence or collection (These frames provide a logical outline for students' talking.)
- their interpretations, their reactions, connections they've made (with other texts, the world, or their own lives), and conclusions they've drawn

It's important to keep in mind that most categories (in either genre) for retelling information will be represented when the student is reading a complete selection, but some will not apply when he's reading an excerpt. In that case I record NA, as previously noted, on the retelling checklist.

When aware of what they should be prepared to talk about, students read actively—with purpose—and coherently express their thinking in the retelling. The exemplars and practice I provide in class simplify these detailed lists of what to tell in a retelling.

Written Retellings: Models in the World

I also like to present examples of retellings found outside of school. For example, we examine the summaries on the insides of book jackets and the reviews on their back covers. Newspapers' and publishers' book reviews are another source of exemplars. I point out that even though these professional retellings are based on

Name: _____ Date _____

Selection: _____

Ask the student to retell what was read as if you haven't heard it before. When there are pauses, use the phrase "Anything else?" to prompt the student to tell more. Students' demonstrated understanding before questioning is considered independent and unassisted. If the reader needs the assistance of teacher probing and questioning to relate his thinking, the retelling is assisted. Place a Y or an N in the column to indicate whether a criterion was addressed. Place an A or a U in the column to indicate whether the reader's retelling of that area was assisted or unassisted. Give examples to explain and add any comments that would clarify scoring. Use the rubric to give an overall score for this retelling and an overall combined score for the word reading and the retelling. **Record NA if the passage was not read orally.**

Skill	Y/N	Assisted/ Unassisted	Examples	Comments
Retold gist (main idea and significant details)				
Identified key terms or new vocabulary in the passage				
Retelling followed text's structure (e.g., description, sequence, compare, cause and effect)				
Shared personal interpretations				
Interpreted visuals and/or graphic aids				
Made connections (to self, to other text, to the world)				
Described personal reactions				

continued

figure 4–3 Retelling with Expository Text

Skill	Y/N	Assisted/ Unassisted	Examples	Comments
Evaluated the quality of the text				
Explained logical conclusions				

Overall, retelling was _____ (score).

Score	Criteria
4 Highly Independent	Highly independent retelling that was full, detailed, and appropriately integrated with personal interpretations.
3 Borderline Independent/ Instructional	Mostly independent retelling that was close to full and detailed. It also included some personal interpretations.
2 Instructional	Mostly assisted retelling. With probing and questioning, the retelling included details and personal interpretation at a satisfactory (acceptable) level.
1 Frustrational	Even with the assistance of probing and questions, the retelling was fragmented and disjointed.

The overall level for this passage (considering both word-reading accuracy and retelling) is shown below. (Refer to the split-level guide for this scoring. **Record NA if the passage retold was not read orally**.)

_____	4	Independent
_____	3	Borderline Independent/Instructional
_____	2	Instructional
_____	1	Frustrational

Comments

figure 4–3 Continued

© 2006 by Mary Shea. From *Where's the Glitch? How to Use Running Records with Older Readers, Grades 5–8.* Portsmouth, NH: Heinemann.

Name: _____ Date _____

Selection: _____

Ask the student to retell what was read as if you haven't heard it before. When there are pauses, use the phrase "Anything else?" to prompt the student to tell more. Students' demonstrated understanding before questioning is considered independent and unassisted. If the reader needs the assistance of teacher probing and questioning to relate his thinking, the retelling is assisted. Place a Y or an N in the column to indicate whether a criterion was addressed. Place an A or a U in the column to indicate whether the reader's retelling of that area was assisted or unassisted. Give examples to explain and add any comments that would clarify scoring. Use the rubric to give an overall score for this retelling and an overall combined score for the word reading and the retelling. **Record NA if the passage was not read orally.**

Skill	Y/N	Assisted/ Unassisted	Examples	Comments
Retold gist (main idea and significant details)				
Used terms or vocabulary in the passage/poem				
Retelling included narrative/poetic elements revealed in passage/poem (setting, plot, figurative language, etc.)				
Shared personal interpretations				
Interpreted visuals or clues offered by author (e.g., fore-shadowing)				
Made connections (to self, to other text, to the world)				
Described personal reactions				

continued

figure 4-4 Retelling with a Narrative Text or Poem

Skill	Y/N	Assisted/ Unassisted	Examples	Comments
Evaluated the quality of the text				
Explained logical conclusions				

Overall, retelling was _____ (score).

Score	Criteria
4 Highly Independent	Highly independent retelling that was full, detailed, and appropriately integrated with personal interpretations.
3 Borderline Independent/ Instructional	Mostly independent retelling that was close to full and detailed. It also included some personal interpretations.
2 Instructional	Mostly assisted retelling. With probing and questioning, the retelling included details and personal interpretation at a satisfactory (acceptable) level.
1 Frustrational	Even with the assistance of probing and questions, the retelling was fragmented and disjointed.

The overall level for this passage (considering both word-reading accuracy and retelling) is shown below. (Refer to the split-level guide for this scoring. **Record NA if the passage retold was not read orally**.)

_____ 4   Independent
_____ 3   Borderline Independent/Instructional
_____ 2   Instructional
_____ 1   Frustrational

Comments

figure 4–4 Continued

© 2006 by Mary Shea. From *Where's the Glitch? How to Use Running Records with Older Readers, Grades 5–8*. Portsmouth, NH: Heinemann.

a whole book rather than a one-minute read, their content parallels what students need to include in MRR retellings.

Retelling Demonstrations: Showing and Practicing the Process

At this point, my students know what is required for a quality retell; they're eager to give it a try. But before they do, I want to *show* them how all of these steps go together.

Teacher Modeling

I model a one-minute read followed by a retelling, guiding the transfer of concepts students have learned from whole-text, real-world examples of retelling to the MRR situation. I tape the reading and retelling so students have an opportunity to replay and verify what I've said. Listening to the recording seems to lessen students' anxiety or reactivity about being taped themselves. With subsequent examples, I retell something I've read silently, again taping my retelling. I clearly demonstrate that I'm using the Guidelines for a Retelling chart for cues (Figure 4–2). With each sample, I collaboratively evaluate my retelling with the students, using the appropriate checklist (Figure 4–3 or 4–4).

Since this is their first experience with scoring, I ask them to just think about the chart as they listen to me talk. When I've finished retelling, I initiate a discussion about my performance. I ask them which criteria I met. Of course, I expect students to justify the scores they give me. Criteria I've met are scored Y (yes) and then U (unassisted) because I did the retelling on my own. I scribe their evaluations and comments on a transparency of the checklist. When necessary we determine if any unaddressed criteria really need to be marked NA. Then we begin to examine what I didn't tell.

I draw students' attention to areas that I missed. I teach them to probe me for my thinking in these areas and then decide whether my responses fulfill the criteria. I want to use prompts that don't give away the information they seek. My students ask, "Anything else?" or "What makes you say that?" (Benson and Cummins 2000). We discuss disagreements until we come to a consensus. I'm scored Y for a criterion if they're satisfied that my response meets it, but A (assisted) in the next column because I needed the assistance of their prompt. In this practice the overall level for the passage isn't evaluated since the focus was solely on the retelling. (See Figure 4–5 for a sample checklist based on a teacher model.)

Name: **Teacher Model**   Date _____

Selection: *The Route to Freedom,* by James Oliver Norton

Ask the student to retell what was read as if you haven't heard it before. When there are pauses, use the phrase "Anything else?" to prompt the student to tell more. Students' demonstrated understanding before questioning is considered independent and unassisted. If the reader needs the assistance of teacher probing and questioning to relate his thinking, the retelling is assisted. Place a Y or an N in the column to indicate whether a criterion was addressed. Place an A or a U in the column to indicate whether the reader's retelling of that area was assisted or unassisted. Give examples to explain and add any comments that would clarify scoring. Use the rubric to give an overall score for this retelling and an overall combined score for the word reading and the retelling. **Record NA if the passage was not read orally.**

Skill	Y/N	Assisted/ Unassisted	Examples	Comments
Retold gist (main idea and significant details)	Y	U		Clear expression of theme. Three relevant details were given.
Identified key terms or new vocabulary in the passage	Y	U		Named terms used with Underground Railroad (e.g., *rails, stations, conductor*)
Retelling followed text's structure (e.g., description, sequence, compare, cause and effect)	Y	A	Left out part about how the UR started but could explain it when asked.	
Shared personal interpretations	Y	A	When asked what she thought about Quakers and their beliefs, she responded.	None noted without prompting.
Interpreted visuals and/or graphic aids	Y	U	Used word box to find out what *guerilla* meant during the time of the UR.	
Made connections (to self, to other text, to the world)	Y	U	Explained that she heard of another explanation of how the name UR came to be. It was connected to a runaway who seemed to vanish and some said he disappeared on an UR.	

continued

figure 4–5 Retelling Checklist for Teacher Model: Retelling with Expository Text

Skill	Y/N	Assisted/ Unassisted	Examples	Comments
Described personal reactions	Y	U	Said that she hadn't realized that people were helping to free slaves even during the Revolution time.	
Evaluated the quality of the text	Y	U	Thought the text was clear and easy to understand.	
Explained logical conclusions	Y	U	Said she can understand why it came to be known as a UR and explained her thinking.	

Overall, retelling was 3 (score).

Score	Criteria
4 Highly Independent	Highly independent retelling that was full, detailed, and appropriately integrated with personal interpretations.
3 Borderline Independent/ Instructional	Mostly independent retelling that was close to full and detailed. It also included some personal interpretations.
2 Instructional	Mostly assisted retelling. With probing and questioning, the retelling included details and personal interpretation at a satisfactory (acceptable) level.
1 Frustrational	Even with the assistance of probing and questions, the retelling was fragmented and disjointed.

The overall level for this passage (considering both word-reading accuracy and retelling) is shown below. (Refer to the split-level guide for this scoring. **Record NA if the passage retold was not read orally.**)

NA	4	Independent
_____	3	Borderline Independent/Instructional
_____	2	Instructional
_____	1	Frustrational

Comments

Although the teacher had to be prompted by the class in some areas, the retelling in general was concluded by the class to be full and complete for the part of the selection read.

figure 4–5 Continued

Now I'm ready to move to the next step—practicing with a partner. I want students to be prepared for the constructive conversations (between the reader and a listener) that follow retellings with significant gaps. Are listeners ready to question readers in ways that will effectively probe what's missing in the retelling? Are readers able to use this directed assistance to expand their retelling?

Practicing Partners: Teacher and Student

Opportunities to practice retelling with a peer give students a chance to refine their performance of the task before it's used as a benchmark or formative assessment. Additionally, the listener's analysis of a peer's retelling informs her own practice. Listeners' feedback includes compliments that encourage retellers and comments that focus their attention on areas for improvement (Koskinen et al. 1988).

Before students begin to practice retelling, I provide one more modeling step. I demonstrate with a student. Observing me working with a classmate offers students an opportunity to negotiate the meaning expressed and the meaning missed; it requires them to listen carefully and critically. Partners experience the possibility of multiple interpretations of a text and the rationales that support various opinions (Brown and Cambourne 1998).

I ask for a volunteer to work with me in front of the class. We each silently read a passage for one minute. Then I begin to retell using the cue chart while my partner listens and evaluates. We also tape-record my retelling. My partner has a checklist attached to a clipboard and scores areas addressed in my retelling as I talk. She prompts me to go on when I pause. When I finish telling, my partner asks me follow-up questions to probe incomplete or inaccurate responses. If my response then fulfills the criterion for an area, she places a Y to indicate that the retell for that item met the criterion and then records an A to note that I had to be assisted. When we finish our conversation, my partner shares her assessment. If I disagree with her scoring, we can play the tape to check and verify. We also revisit the text as we check information and interpretations. Rereading deepens our shared understanding (Temple et al. 2005). After enough practice, partners may determine whether each other's retelling was full and complete, satisfactory, or fragmented. Fortified with examples, students are ready to try retelling in dyads.

Practicing Partners: Peer Dyads

Assign partners who read at similar instructional levels to work together. Robb (2000) notes that students are better able to support each other when the text is at the appropriate level for both. Have students read a text silently for one minute and then retell it to a partner. Tape retellings as students talk. According to Wood (1987), retelling to a partner capitalizes on the inherent pleasure that comes from discussing newly acquired information with a friend. You can synchronize the reading so that everyone is reading during the same minute. Since the retelling with recording will take different amounts of time for different pairs, students who finish their full MRR early can continue reading the rest of the passage. When partners switch roles, they use a different section of the text. While partners practice, I circulate, eavesdrop, and interject my help where needed.

I make sure to stay close to struggling readers, ready to slide in with additional support as I circulate to coach this practice. Dyad members score each other's retelling using the checklists (see Figures 4–3 and 4–4). I have pairs share their experiences and scores with the class. We use these examples to analyze readers' strengths and confusions. The latter become the fodder for whole-class or small-group minilessons where we examine the factors that contribute to or interfere with successful retelling.

Collaborative Analysis of Retellings

It's important to examine the sources of strengths and weaknesses in order to enhance the first and ameliorate the latter. My students and I talk about where and why meaning broke down when reading a particular text. I stress that identifying a problem and its source is the first step to fixing it. I want them to believe that the locus of control for success is within them. That knowledge empowers!

Irwin (1991) reports that experiences, levels of competence, self-confidence, and other factors influence retellings. To identify a glitch, students ask themselves questions that relate to the following factors.

- *Schema (background knowledge) on the topic.* Do I need more information on the topic in order to understand this text? Will rereading or talking about it help me understand new concepts presented by the author?
- *Level of listening (words understood when heard) and/or sight vocabulary.* Were there lots of words I've never heard of in this selection?
- *Cultural differences.* Is this about a way of thinking or pattern of acting that's different from mine?
- *Word-recognition skills.* Can I figure out hard or unfamiliar words?
- *Comfort with the task.* Am I worried about doing well?
- *Responses to environmental influences inside and outside of school.* Am I confident I can be successful?

An analysis of the full MRR yields clues related to these factors and others that enhance or inhibit readers' successful learning with texts. Once we've identified possible glitches with a high degree of specificity, we're more likely to address them efficiently.

Conclusion: Persistence Pays Off

School readers, overly conditioned to the Q-and-A format, may initially balk at retelling. They're uncomfortable with and confused about the expectations for this task that requires more from them. But we know that retelling reveals what the reader considers important in the text as well as his thinking and personal meaning making; it's a window into the reader's mental processing of the text (Roe, Stoodt-Hill, and Burns 2004). But, what we *see* in the performance is highly affected by the teller's ability to use language for sharing ideas. It's not surprising that as students learn about and engage in retelling, their ability to express thoughts clearly and convincingly grows.

Additional side effects of the retelling's verbal rehearsal include

- increased reflection on the content of readings,
- improved overall understanding of what is read, and
- facility with expressing one's ideas. (Koskinen et al. 1988)

And, as students become comfortable with verbal rehearsal and defense of ideas, I've found concurrent improvement in their ability to coherently express their thoughts in writing. They're more aware of what they want to say. They're also more aware of audience and the need to logically organize ideas and express them cogently. This is a giant step and a huge bonus!

Now practice scoring retelling with the CD scripts and recordings. After following along with the models, try scoring on your own. Compare your markings with those of a colleague.

5

Analyzing MRR Results

Data that are gathered simply for the sake of filling folders or checking off demands contribute little to ensure that the next instructional step takes the student where she needs to go. What's the point of having scored MRRs if they're not analyzed—actually autopsied—for sources of glitches? That's the only way to start *what if* thinking—what if we use this or that instructional intervention to scaffold for success? Teachers analyze data from ongoing assessments like MRRs to consider an important question: "What's most important to teach [task/activity] at this moment for this child to move him [the student] forward?" (Routman 2003, 107).

Procedurally, I start by analyzing the target performance—comprehension. Full and deep understanding is always the bottom line; it requires putting all other skills and strategies to work harmoniously and purposefully. Accurate word reading of a passage is of little value without meaning construction. It would be like saying a string of words without any purpose other than correct recitation. I use the retelling to determine the quality of a student's comprehension *with* texts.

Global Indicators of Successful Retelling

At a macro or global level, a successful retelling reflects personally constructed meaning, flows smoothly, makes logical sense in content and sequence, and is filled with text details that support its central ideas (Routman 2003). I assess how fully the reader can *share, clarify,* and *justify* her understanding of the text (Brown and Cambourne, 1998)—expectations I have when listening to anyone present her thinking.

While many assessment tasks are new behaviors or require the demonstration of skills in ways that differ from their use in everyday school activities or daily life, retelling is actually not a new performance demand. It's a well-established outside-of-school linguistic activity—one that varies from brief, to circuitous, to expansive, and, sometimes, even to messy (Brown and Cambourne, 1998). "The function and form of 'telling about' is a long-established feature of most people's verbal repertoires" (25). This doesn't mean that a good retelling is free of *ums* or *ahs*, pauses, backtracking, or short segues to add personal comments and connections.

Think about the last time you told a friend about a great book you read—one he just had to get and read immediately. Or how about telling about the latest hit movie you saw and he didn't. Your retelling is spontaneous; it's first-draft oral writing. I try to remember Anne Lamott's characterization of unrevised first drafts as words "bounding along like huskies across the snow . . . The right words and sentences just do not come pouring out like ticker tape most of the time" (1994, 22). Figure 5–1 shows the text a student read, her initial unassisted retelling, and the teacher's probes to stimulate more telling. Note the first-draft quality of the retelling as Jayne pauses, comments, connects, and *ums* her way through.

But within Jayne's shower of talk, I find indicators of understanding and leads for probing. The teacher's questions are designed to draw Jayne's attention to significant details. Tompkins (2001) refers to this probing of missed details as guiding a *close reading,* but here it's a *close retelling.* Sometimes these details foreshadow or lay the foundation for information that follows in the remainder of the selection. Overlooking their significance often limits the depth of the reader's comprehension.

It's important to pose questions that stimulate a genuine conversation. Notice the exchange full of rich replies that follows Jayne's retelling. There's further evidence of comprehension in this conversation, indication of Jayne's ability to participate in literate discourse, self-revision of her thinking, and making new connections that have emerged from talking. I found that, once the students and I are comfortable with the retelling process, there's a spontaneous flow of genuine questions. Before we reach that level, I use the standard questions for extending a sparse retelling that are suggested in Figure 4–1.

However, a caveat is that I must *customize* questions to the specific selection and pose them in a conversational tone if I wish to effectively assess the reader's global understanding.

When the retelling reflects limited or inaccurate understanding—when there's a gap in the sharing, clarifying, or justifying even with probing questions—I examine a number of factors at the micro level.

Lighting Made Easy
Rayvon Fouche

Each time you flip on a light switch or a lamp, you're making a connection to Lewis H. Latimer, a foremost inventor and draftsman of electrical technology from its early days. Latimer was born in Chelsea, Massachusetts, in 1848, six years after his parents, former slaves George and Rebecca Latimer, escaped to freedom from Norfolk, Virginia. Besides attending Phillips Grammar School in Boston, Latimer spent much time working in his father's barbershop. He also worked odd jobs such as hanging wallpaper and selling the abolitionist newspaper *The Liberator* to help support his family.

When Lewis decided to enlist in the U.S. Navy in 1864, the Civil War was already in its third year. On September 13, he was assigned to the *Ohio* as a landsman and served until July 3, 1865, at which time the Navy honorably discharged him from the *Massasoit*.

Jayne's Retelling

J: I read the beginning of an article titled "Lighting Made Easy." Ah . . . it . . . it was about a man named Lewis Latimer. Um . . . um . . . Latimer was an inventor. Um . . . He must have worked on light switches and lamps. [*Pause*] . . . Uh . . . because it said that when you use these you're making a connection to him. Uh . . . light switches to turn on lights and lamps do make lighting up rooms and outside at night easy. [*Pause*] Ah . . . it said he was a draftsman too. I've heard that word, but I'm not sure what that job is. Um . . . ah . . . he was born in Massachusetts in 18-something. It said his parents were slaves. But, he went to school . . . um . . . um . . . so he got an education. He worked in a barbershop. Uh . . . he hung wallpaper and sold newspapers too. [*Pause*] . . . Oh yeah . . . it was an abolitionist newspaper . . . um . . . and . . . and those were the people who helped slaves escape on the Underground Railroad. [*Pause*] So he might have . . . uh . . . been in . . . like working with them. Latimer joined the navy during the Civil War. Uh . . . it told which ships he was on and what his job was, . . . um . . . but I didn't know what it was because I never heard of that job.

I expect it will tell how he started to invent light switches and lamps to make lighting things up easy. Um . . . they had to use gas lamps in those days or candles maybe. So inventing electrical things must have been a big deal.

T: You explained quite a bit, Jayne. You were really thinking while reading. The article did say that he worked as a draftsman. You've heard that word but don't know what that is?

J: Right.

T: It's a person who makes drawings of machine structures. You mentioned that you predict the article will tell how he invented light switches. Why do you think that?

J: Because of the title and first sentence.

continued

figure 5–1 Jayne's Retelling

T: How would his work as a draftsman help him with electrical inventions like switches and lamps?

J: Well, when you invent things you have to draw pictures of it exactly—like what it looks like and how to make it—kinda like exact diagrams or scale drawings. It would be like the direction pages you get to put something you buy together . . . I guess. So, knowing how to draw like that would be important when you invent things. You have to show your work. Then you get the rights—or something like that—to make it and nobody can copy you and you get money for the invention.

T: I believe the rights are called a *patent*. It comes from the government and it documents that you're the inventor.

The navy job you didn't know was landsman. He served in the navy as a landsman. I checked this because I haven't heard it before either. The dictionary said it was a person who was an inexperienced sailor.

J: He must not have had a lot of experiences on boats when he was growing up. He must have picked the navy to join because he wanted to go to sea or it seemed better than fighting in the army. I'd think it would be kinda safer than fighting at Gettysburg; that was a real bloody battle.

T: Was his life better than his parents' life?

J: Yeah.

T: Why do you think so?

J: They had been slaves. But they escaped and got to Massachusetts where they didn't allow slavery. They must have gotten jobs to earn a living for their family. Latimer got an education in school.

T: Yes, we're told that his father had a business; the barbershop that Latimer worked in was his father's. You're right; it did tell us that Latimer went to *grammar* school. Do you know what a grammar school is and what that tells us about how far he went with his school education?

J: I'm not sure.

T: A grammar school usually includes grades kindergarten through 8.

J: So, he didn't finish high school? He must have been smart and learned a lot of things in the navy and on his own.

T: I'd agree with you about that. I've enjoyed discussing this with you, Jayne. We learned a lot in that little bit of text about this man. You can read the rest of the article to find out how events in his life led to his work as an inventor.

figure 5–1 Continued

What Else Is Analyzed? Looking from Macro to Micro Aspects

Data from any retelling yield a myriad of evidence to add to those collected in the ebb and flow of daily classroom activities. However, the data aren't collected solely to document learning; they've also collected to direct instruction. When I allow what I learn during the MRR to guide me, I'm better able to differentiate instruction to meet learners' needs.

Some evidence is obvious. Some requires checking extraneous variables related to the environment, the materials used, or the reader's background knowledge, confidence, and facility with language. I consider whether

- The reader didn't understand what was expected in a retelling or was not comfortable with the task.
- The reader appeared to lack experience in telling about, or expressive language skills, inhibiting a clear demonstration of his understanding and thinking.
- The concepts presented were difficult for this reader. Did the reader lack background knowledge on the topic?
- The text was frustrational (too hard) for the reader. Perhaps it contained too many technical words that the reader didn't know. Maybe several non-technical words in the selection were simply not part of this reader's vocabulary.
- The reading was choppy with many starts and stops. Did the reader lack fluency in the sense of smoothness (rather than speed)? Building fluency is discussed further in Chapter 6. For now, it's important to note whether the student made the oral reading sound like talking with regard to phrasing, expression, and intonation. I want to note here that when I consider whether the reader was *expressive*, I'm not expecting a budding drama queen or a new Chris Rock. I am looking for natural tone and voice modulation, words appropriately chunked into meaningful phrases, and a steady rhythmic pace that emphasized and adjusted to the meaning the reader was constructing *with this passage*. Appropriate pace is highly passage specific; it's customized situation by situation. It's *just right* with regard to speed for each passage. The reader picks up speed, slows down, and flows along (in between fast and slow) as he engages with the author and the information. Pace is associated with reading fluency; Chapter 6 discusses all aspects of fluency. Calculating words read correctly per minute, or WCPM (words correct per minute), for an indication of fluency doesn't consider students' ability to *strategically* pace their reading. For example, good readers adjust pace when they're confused and when they attempt to correct errors.

I also analyze how a reader responds to support in the form of encouragement or scaffolding that dances to what Cole (2004) calls a *micro-macro tango*—drawing attention to large concepts (gist) and details (sentences and words) that have immediate importance or portent. I wonder whether the reader can take my lead and run with it.

In-the-Moment Feedback

Throughout the MRR, I'm scaffolding and encouraging *on the run* as I assess—and sometimes intuit—the reader's needs. I'm listening attentively to ensure an accurate recording of the event, but I'm always listening diagnostically to determine how I can support the reader without influencing the data. Like *Pinocchio*'s Jiminy Cricket, I'm sitting on the reader's shoulder, whispering kudos or general reminders whenever she falters—"Just use the strategies you know to figure this out. You can do it." However comfortable I make the interaction, I know some readers are still aware that this is a performance demand and need reassurance. It reminds me of how I feel when being observed by a supervisor or colleague as I teach. The ole butterflies-in-the-stomach feeling is a sign that we're serious about giving a performance that will illuminate our skills.

Debriefing: Sharing Results with the Reader

Even though we typically have an idea of how well we performed a task—as registered on our *internal success meter*—we still enjoy compliments from others; we also expect and appreciate sensitively offered, constructive suggestions from an audience. My students are no different. I want them to begin to rely on their own success meter—to hear its message, accept what it indicates, and positively plan for improvement. But, I also respond to their need for an outside opinion of their performance. After a brief pat on the reader's back, the debriefing begins with the reader's self-reflection and continues with my comments. Together we sum up our integrated conclusions to discern a next best step forward.

Compliments: What Went Well?

When the reader has completed the reading and retelling, we share compliments and comments, in that order. I start by sharing a brief compliment about the performance. Then I ask the reader to respond to what I've said and serve the next volley in the interaction. I want him to compliment his own reading. This eases the tension and gets the conversation started. At first, readers tend to start with a negative. It seems to be a natural human reaction; they put their errors on the table and show the observer (me) they've recognized what didn't go well. In the beginning I have to insist and even help them start acknowledging what went well. They're too modest, too hesitant to toot their own horn. I want them to look at what's in the glass half (or even less) full; I never allow students to beat themselves up!

I might begin with something like this: "You were working very hard with this section. You shared a lot of information in your retelling." Although the conversation will get to decoding, I want the reader to begin with a focus on the target outcome, which is always comprehension. I say, "First, tell me what worked well for you as you tried to understand what this passage was all about."

The reader downloads his thinking. Then I respond. Next, I tell him what I think went well and ask for his reactions to these observations. My comments are connected to comprehension even when the performance aspect we discuss was linked initially to decoding. For example, I might say, "I noticed that you reread in some places and that helped you figure out a word or understand the sentence better." Or I might say, "I noticed that when you didn't know a word you put in a synonym that made sense in the sentence. It seemed like you used the context to decide what word would work. That was very effective because you continued to understand what the passage was about. You knew that you could find out about the word you didn't know after you finished the reading." After that, we move on to identifying possible glitches.

Comments: What Caused Glitches?

After discussing what we both thought went well, I say, "Now, tell me what parts seemed difficult." We explore whatever the reader brings up, whether it's related to comprehension or decoding. Then I bring up one or two points that I'd like to focus on. That's quite enough. After any more than one or two teaching points, students become overwhelmed and tune out! They're on overload; they're also discouraged about having too much to fix. I select significant glitches that we can work on right now; remaining glitches are fodder for future lessons. Surprisingly, some of today's glitches get corrected naturally as readers practice with more reading, discuss text content, listen to others, and engage in daily learning activities. And I may plan lessons to eradicate observed glitches we never talked about.

There may also be times when I don't have additional significant errors to bring up—what the reader identified was sufficient. Regardless of how many particular areas of confusion we discuss, the conversation isn't solely focused on *corrective* feedback—feedback that corrects mistakes or supplies answers and explanations. My feedback is also intended to feed forward, building scaffolds that will promote and sustain readers' success in future readings. I want to ease them toward independence, secure with the tools they need to build and maintain a literate life. Know-how and the right tools make a task doable and the worker confident.

Feeding Forward: Setting Goals

I use the post-MRR conversation in a way that values learning from mistakes. The reader and I talk about the reading performance just discussed with a vision toward the future. I suggest a strategy that would have worked where confusion reigned, explain how that strategy works, and model its use, step by step, in this situation. Then we plan on practicing the strategy in daily readings. In this way, my feedback is feeding forward, building a path for success in the reader's next encounter with text.

Quantifying and Qualifying Results

When my conversation with the reader wraps up, I lead her into the activity I'd like her to resume or direct her to where she should go. For example, I might say, "Thanks, Beth, for doing this reading with me. Now we can decide what to do next to ensure your success with the materials we're using in class. I want you to think about being ready to *unpack your thinking* in our discussions. I want you to tell everything you know about what you've read—including information from the passage *and* your ideas. Now you can work on whatever you've brought to study hall (or return to your study hall, or work on homework until the late bus is called)." Once Beth leaves, I'm ready to tally and quantify results.

Scoring the Retelling

I analyze the pattern of my markings on the retelling checklist to consider the level of this text for this reader *at this time*. The levels are very tentative. Just as readers outgrow clothes when physical changes occur, they outgrow lower levels of text as they build reading skills.

The three levels of text for any reader include *independent, instructional,* and *frustrational.* They relate to the reader's ability to read a text *with understanding.*

- The independent level indicates that the reader can *independently* read the text with full and deep understanding.

- The instructional level indicates that the reader *needs instruction* or assistance from the teacher (or another competent person) to read and understand the text.
- The frustrational level means that this text is just *too hard* right now. The reader cannot read and understand it even with help. (Shea 2000)

These levels are sensitive to personal factors (variables) such as the reader's background knowledge, interest in the content, and motivation to read this text. They're also affected by the classroom tone and the amount of support others provide the reader as well as cues within the text (e.g., charts, definitions of words, pictures). Combined, these variables have a significant influence in determining a reader's level with a particular passage—much more than the text difficulty (e.g., grade levels) calculated from readability formulas. These factors also make the levels very fluid; it's conceivable that a reader might read at the independent level on one seventh-grade text, at the instructional level on another, and at frustional level on a third. To determine where the reader's performance fell with the text he just read and retold, I examine my notations on the checklist I used for recording.

If most or all of my checks are in the unassisted retelling column and the telling for those parts was thorough, I score the retell as *full and complete.* "Full and complete" indicates that the text was at the reader's independent level. If most or many of the checks for acceptable retelling are in the assisted column, I score the retelling as *satisfactory.* For this score, the reader can have one or two checks in the unassisted column or have one (not more) area where he could not retell at all. "Satisfactory" indicates that the text was at the reader's instructional level. If the reader can talk only about a minimal portion of the text, even with assistance, and I have a lot of blank areas on my checklist, I score the overall retelling as *fragmented.* "Fragmented" indicates that this text was at the reader's frustrational level.

Retelling Score	Retelling Level	Description of Retelling
4	Independent (can read independently)	Highly independent retelling that was full, detailed, and appropriately integrated with personal interpretations.
3	Borderline between Independent and Instructional (can mostly read by herself; needs minimal questioning)	Mostly independent retelling that was close to full and detailed. It also included some personal interpretations.

Retelling Score	Retelling Level	Description of Retelling
2	Instructional (can read with help)	Mostly assisted retelling. With probing and questioning, the retelling included details and personal interpretation at a satisfactory (acceptable) level.
1	Frustrational (it's too hard right now)	Even with the assistance of probing and questions, the retelling was fragmented and disjointed.

With a level established for the retelling, I have half of a full picture; I have a measure of the reader's meaning processing with this text. But that's not enough; I also need to know how accurately the reader processed the words. If the reader retold without being able to process (read) words accurately, the retelling was probably based on background knowledge rather than meaning construction with this passage.

Determining Oral Reading Accuracy

To determine the reader's success with word processing, I first add up the miscues that were not self-corrected. Self-corrected miscues are no longer counted as errors. Figure 3–1 provides a guide for identifying what counts as an error.

Then I count the number of words in the passage up to the point where the reader stopped reading. Numbers (e.g., *2005, 52, 107*) count as one word; acronyms (e.g., *U.S.*) count as one word. Next, I subtract the total number of errors from the number of words read to determine the total number of words read accurately. Finally, I divide the total number of words read correctly by the total number of words in the passage up to the point where the reader stopped reading. This gives me a percent of word-reading accuracy.

total number of words up to the point where the reader stopped reading = 137

total number of errors = 7

total number of words read correctly = 137 − 7 = 130

$$\frac{130 \text{ (total number of words read correctly)}}{137 \text{ (total number of words up to the point where the reader stopped reading)}}$$

.948 × 100 = 94.8 = 95% word-reading accuracy

With the calculated percent for word-reading accuracy, I refer to the following chart to determine the reader's word-processing level with this text. I determine whether the score falls within the independent, instructional, or frustrational level (Clay 1993; Shea 2000).

Level of Oral Reading	Word-Reading Accuracy
Independent (can read independently)	95% to 100%
Instructional (can read with help)	90% to 94%
Frustrational (it's too hard right now)	below 90%

I can also use the error count when determining an *error rate*. As an aspect of fluency, the error rate indicates the *frequency of interruptions* in the flow of reading. Minimally interrupted reading flow, or smoothness, is important, but it's not the sole indicator of reading fluency. Other critical aspects of fluent reading are discussed in Chapter 6.

Calculating the Error Rate

The error rate is an estimate of the number of words a student read correctly before his flow was interrupted by a miscue. It's easily calculated by dividing the total number of words in the passage up to the point where the reader stopped reading by the total number of errors.

$$\frac{\text{total number of words in the passage up to the point the reader stopped reading}}{\text{total number of errors}}$$

Using the numbers from the previous example for calculating the percent of word-reading accuracy, I'd compute the following:

$$\frac{137}{7} = 19.57 = 20 \text{ (rounded to the nearest whole number)}$$

The answer indicates that the flow of reading in this performance was interrupted by, approximately, one error every twentieth word. With such an error rate, a reader would have accurately processed a reasonable amount of content before his flow was disturbed. It's not a guarantee, but it's easier to process meaning when errors infrequently interrupt the reading flow. An error rate of 20 allows a reader to process a sentence or two before hitting a bump in the road. And some errors don't even significantly change meaning. All errors are not created equal, even though they're equally counted as errors.

Errors That Change Meaning and Errors That Don't

As previously noted, readers often make errors that don't matter with regard to understanding the overall meaning or even specific details in a text. Young children embellish simple text with background knowledge or ideas gained from illustrations. Sometimes readers overuse background knowledge, reading what they expect to be on the page. Good readers effectively substitute a synonym for an unknown word. Considering significant and insignificant miscues in the overall analysis is discussed in Chapter 7.

Putting the Pieces Together

I now have two separately established levels—one for word-reading accuracy and another for retelling as an indication of comprehension—that I want to integrate for a complete picture of the reader's performance with this text. I use Leslie and Caldwell's (2001) split levels of performance to determine the reader's *overall* reading level with this text at this time. The chart in Figure 5–2 shows how the

Word-Reading Accuracy	Comprehension (Retelling)	Overall Level	Score
Independent ⟶	Independent ⟶	Independent	4
Independent ⟶	Borderline Independent to Instructional ⟶	Borderline Independent (with observation)	3
Independent ⟶	Instructional ⟶	Instructional	2
Independent ⟶	Frustrational ⟶	Frustrational	1
Instructional ⟶	Independent ⟶	Instructional	3
Instructional ⟶	Borderline Independent to Instructional ⟶	Instructional	2
Instructional ⟶	Instructional ⟶	Instructional	2
Instructional ⟶	Frustrational ⟶	Frustrational	1
Frustrational ⟶	Independent ⟶	Instructional (with observation)	2
Frustrational ⟶	Borderline Independent to Instructional ⟶	Instructional (with observation)	2
Frustrational ⟶	Instructional ⟶	Frustrational	1
Frustrational ⟶	Frustrational ⟶	Frustrational	1

(Adapted from Leslie and Caldwell 2001; Shea 2000)

figure 5–2 Split Levels of Reading Performance

overall level is determined. Note that comprehension weighs very heavily. For example, a passage scored at the independent level on word-reading accuracy but as frustrational on comprehension is frustrational overall. Comprehension trumps word-reading accuracy. Without understanding, it's word calling, not reading.

Figure 5–3 shows a student's oral reading sample. Notice how the student's retelling evolves into discourse as the teacher nudges her to elaborate and clarify. Readers who have processed the text fluently are more likely to retell in ways that are full and complete, sharing the surface and deep understanding they have. So there's still another measure to record on the form: fluency. This adds detail to the current snapshot of the reader's performance.

Count of words in passage up to point when reading stopped = 158 (Note: The initial *R.* counts as a word; *24* counts as a word; *300* counts as a word; *1859* counts as a word.)

Our Dependence on Oil
by R. Anthony Kugler

If you live in the United States, chances are very good that you have ridden in a car within the past 24 hours. More than 300 million automobiles exist in this country, and all of them consume an increasingly limited and costly substance: petroleum, commonly known as oil. But oil does more than keep traffic moving on the highways. We also use it to heat and cool our homes in winter, to make products like plastics and pesticides, and to bring the food grown with the help of those pesticides to our supermarkets. Oil, in short, is responsible for many of the advances and conveniences we tend to take for granted—and for some of our most serious problems.

Although ancient peoples all over the world knew about small surface deposits of oil, sometimes using it as a medicine, it was not until 1859 that large-scale production became possible.

Retelling
J: I started reading an article that tells how we depend on oil. They keep saying that's what's making gas prices get higher and higher. Because we have to depend on Iraq and places near there for our oil and they can charge us more for it because we don't have oil like they do and we need what they have.

T: Whoa—just a minute, Jason. It seems like you're making a good personal connection, but you're not being clear. Who's the *they* who "keep saying," and what's the *that* "that's making gas prices higher"?

J: *They* are reporters or, maybe, newspaper writers. It's because other countries like Iraq have what we need and we don't have any or, maybe, a little bit. That's the *that* that's making gas prices higher. We have to depend on them because we have only a little bit and they can get lots of money from us.

continued

---

figure 5–3 Student's Oral Reading Sample

T: OK, I understand what you mean now. Go on. What else?

J: In the United States there are millions of cars on the road and they need lots of gas. And that's [gas] made from oil. Um . . . oil's used for heating homes and for getting food to supermarkets too. There was another thing, but I didn't know that word. I probably said it wrong too.

    Umm . . . for getting food to supermarkets gets back to gasoline because that would be what the gasoline trucks use. Ah . . . oh yeah. It said that oil makes our life convenient, but also causes us problems. Um . . . that's like his [writer] opinion. He'll [author] probably write about why he thinks that way later in the article.

    [*Pause*] Um . . . then it started about long ago. Uh . . . um . . . it said that in ancient days, people used oil as a medicine. I hope they didn't have to drink it! Ugh. Um . . . and they didn't have the machines we have so they didn't need it [oil] like us. And, anyway, they couldn't have gotten oil out of the ground like we do now without drilling machines. [*Longer pause*]

T: Anything else?

J: Ah . . . um . . . no. Um . . . I mean it started to talk about something in 1800-something, but I'm not sure.

T: It said that in 1859, large-scale production of oil became possible. What about that?

J: That means . . . uh . . . like being able to get a lot of oil and then make the gasoline quickly. I think it's going to tell how someone invented something like a drilling machine . . . uh . . . um . . . in that year probably.

T: That's a logical prediction, Jason. The word you wondered about named another product made from the oil. That's *pesticides*. It's right here—*pes-ti-cides*. Have you ever heard of it?

J: I think I've heard it, but I'm not sure what it is.

T: Pesticides are chemicals that are used to destroy plant or animal pests that kill crops. You might have heard about airplanes flying low over crops to spray them with pesticides. The crops are protected, but people worry about eating plants that have been sprayed. There was another product mentioned. Do you remember what it was?

J: Um . . . not really.

T: Oil is used to make plastic. Why would that cause us to be dependent on oil?

J: Ah . . . well, millions of things are made from plastic. Just look around here [the room], for instance. [*Pause*] . . . We might even need oil more for plastic making than for gasoline. Um . . . or close to it!

T: Did the author talk about depending on Iraq and other countries for oil?

J: Ah . . . no, but that's who we depend on to get oil. He's [author] telling how we depend on oil for products we use like uh . . . gas and heat . . . um . . . and plastic. Oh . . . and pes-ti-cides. But I bet he'll talk [about] depending on those countries for it too. That would make sense for dependence on oil.

T: That would make sense, so it's a good prediction about what might be coming up in the article. I wanted to know if you realized that it was your prediction and not what the author actually talked about in the part you read so far.

    Jason, you really kept talking this time. I hardly had to nudge you along. Your retelling showed what you understood and connections you were making. Now, tell me what you think went well in this reading and retelling.

figure 5–3 Continued

Fluency: A Critical Component for Success

Chapter 6 examines the critical components of reading fluency that affect students' ability to smoothly process text (read the words) and make meaning (comprehend). The student's level of fluency with a particular selection is assessed, recorded on the form, and integrated with other data.

6

Fluency

There's much ado about reading *fluency* lately and that's a very good thing. Fluency is a critical component of efficient comprehension and must be taught and practiced (Chard, Vaughn, and Tyler 2002; Kuhn and Stahl 2000). Schreiber (1980) describes how readers gradually move from an accuracy stage, where they recognize words with sustained attention on decoding, to a stage of fluency. The accuracy stage is often characterized by slow, halting, or expressionless reading—behaviors linked to poor comprehension even when word identification is accurate (Rasinski 2000). I'm constantly working to move students quickly and seamlessly beyond accuracy to the fluency—or *accuracy-plus*—stage, where comprehension is easier. But then I need to know what constitutes the *plus* in *accuracy-plus*? What *are* the indicators of fluency? How will I know that readers have achieved it?

Fluency can be assessed through oral readers' accuracy, automatic word recognition, expression, phrasing, intonation, and retellings (Fountas and Pinnell 1996, 2001; Prescott-Griffin and Witherell 2004; Rasinski 2003; Tompkins 2003). Readers who've experienced abundant models of fluent reading are more likely to move into fluent reading effortlessly. When they don't, we need to model, model, model fluency. We help readers recognize fluency's many elements and we plan ample opportunities for them to practice and *feel* fluent. Reading fluency is not the only factor, but it is a significant contributor to readers' understanding of texts. If we are to scaffold their growth toward *real* fluency, we must first understand its critical elements.

I've found a proverbial fly in the ointment. Some definitions of fluency lead to narrow instruction and one-dimensional assessments; they actually inhibit comprehension. The definitions I'm referring to concentrate on reading speed, overemphasizing *words read correctly per minute* (WCPM). The calculation for WCPM is simple; it's the total number of text words read correctly in a one-minute period. Such a focus creates *NASCAR readers*—readers who race through text and call off words as quickly as possible. Too often, NASCAR readers are the ones who have been struggling with texts for a long time. They've come to assume that speed and getting to the finish line as quickly as possible spell success. Their faith is based on a straw definition of reading fluency. When it doesn't work, another hope is shattered.

Although reading rate is a factor, it never guarantees fluency. "Fluent reading is faster [than disfluent] but there are other features to consider as well" (Allington 2001, 71).

What Is Fluency?

Fluency is complex, but it's not a mystery. Fluency is multifaceted; it has several aspects that need to work synchronously. "Fluency results from a complex interrelationship of processes that is more than the sum of these component parts" (Fountas and Pinnell 2001, 316). The components include flow, accuracy, automatic word recognition, phrasing, and prosody (Rasinski 2005).

Flow *is* about speed, but it's not about a race to the last period. Speed in the sense of fastness isn't what I'm looking for. Flow involves smooth, automatic recognition of words. But it's more than that—much more. There's a better way to think about reading pace—a way that conceptually matches how good readers move through text. Flurkey's (1998) suggested comparison of flow to water's movement in a river led me to form a visual. For a glimpse of it, try this: Picture three rivers and decide which is productively in harmony with the environment and accomplishing its purpose.

It's About Flow

A lazily moving river ends up stagnant; debris gets bogged down on its bottom, bacteria flourish, and the water becomes dark, slimy, and murky. A raging river causes havoc, creating a path of destruction with its rush to the sea. Neither of the first two rivers is in harmony with the environment; neither supports life. But a third kind of river accomplishes its purpose while in harmony with all around it.

A smooth, flowing river supports life within and around it as it delivers water to the sea. I want students to move through text like this third kind of river. I'm looking for *flow*. Flow is about pacing or rate variability that's just right; it's also about smoothness of movement (Flurkey 1998). Third-river readers flow through text because they effortlessly recognize most words automatically and less familiar ones with minimal trouble. That doesn't mean they're on cruise control, at one speed. Just like the third river that ripples through straightaways and navigates around a bend in its path, fluent readers hurry along and slow down to accommodate the terrain. In some places there's lots beneath the surface that draws attention. In other places, it's all right to skip along while enjoying the surroundings. Flurkey (1998) found that reading rate varies in effective readings as well as proficient (effective and efficient) ones. He also concluded, "the proficient readings that I've studied showed evidence of greater variability than those readings that were merely efficient" (41).

Third-river readers also accomplish their task; they get to the end of the passage. But on the way these readers have worked in harmony with the author; they've made sense with the text. Appropriate flow allows third-river readers an opportunity to integrate other aspects of fluency as they enjoy the experience and think about the author's message.

It's About Automaticity and Accuracy

Alone, flow is insufficient; fluency also requires *automaticity.* A high level of automatic word recognition (Samuels 2002) and a high level of automatic information processing (Allington 2001) are characteristics of automaticity.

"At its simplest, automaticity refers to the ability to engage and coordinate a number of complex subskills and strategies with little cognitive effort" (Allington 2001, 72). Hudson, Lane, and Pullen (2005) note that when word identification is quick and effortless, more cognitive resources can be devoted to other aspects of fluency—and to comprehension. In other words, automaticity and accuracy grease the gears of fluent readers.

Tompkins emphasizes, "Fluency is the ability to read smoothly and with expression, and in order to read fluently, students must be able to recognize many, many words automatically" (2003, 181). I use an approximate rates of words read correctly per minute as an indicator of students' level of automaticity in word recognition (Rasinski 2005). (See Figure 6–1.) I use other measures for other fluency factors, which are discussed later in this chapter.

Readers whose percent of word-reading accuracy is instructional on grade-level text and whose WCPM is within (or near) expected norms are progressing adequately on these indicators. However, here's a caveat: I use these estimations

Determine the reader's rate on a particular passage by counting the number of *words correctly read per minute* (WCPM). Compare this number to the table estimates for automaticity.

Keep in mind that the oral reading for an MRR is timed for one minute, but the reader is allowed to finish the sentence he's on at that moment. The completion of the sentence enhances comprehension, but it adds more words read after the one-minute point. Make a slash after the word read at the one-minute mark; count words read correctly up to that point for the WCPM count. All words up to the end of the sentence (actual stopping point for oral reading) are used in the calculation of word-reading accuracy and miscue analysis.

Grade	Fall (WCPM)	Winter (WCPM)	Spring (WCPM)
5	80–120	100–140	110–150
6	100–140	110–150	120–160
7	110–150	120–160	130–170
8	120–160	130–170	140–180

figure 6–1 Reading Fluency Target Rate Norms (Rasinski 2005)

cautiously and in conjunction with assessment of other fluency elements as well as the particular demands of the text.

Needless to say, readers also need to be automatically correct in recognizing words. A high number of miscues make the reading disfluent even when there's flow. Proficient readers are able to direct more conscious attention to understanding the text because they're decoding words automatically *and* accurately. But, "accuracy is . . . not enough to produce fluent reading" (Fountas and Pinnell 2001, 316).

Accuracy in word recognition also facilitates the recognition of groups of words, allowing readers to build meaning with phrase and sentence units rather than separate words. Building meaning at the phrase and sentence levels is so much more efficient and less exhausting cognitively.

It's About Phrasing

Appropriate phrasing is central to comprehension because meaning resides in phrases rather than in individual words (Rasinski 2003). Phrase reading facilitates the transfer of information from short- to long-term memory (Tompkins 2003); it also illuminates nonsensical utterances, hopefully stimulating self-initiated reexamination and self-corrections that keep meaning intact. This stringing together of words on the run (while reading) is facilitated by automaticity and accuracy in word recognition.

Fluent readers exhibit an ability to connect words into syntactically meaningful units (phrases and sentences) as they're recognized—or maybe *because* words are decoded accurately and automatically. Phrasing is about *chunking*—stringing together—words into comprehensible units for reading, connecting, and comprehending. Fluent readers chunk as they read, capturing key ideas and connections (Shea 2004).

Good phrasing is hard to define with a simple rule since it's situation specific; it depends on the sentence. But it does appear that fluent readers apply their knowledge of natural breaks for spoken utterances when reading. These are associated with syntactical structures in the sentences (Schreiber 1980). Schreiber suggests that fluent readers initially segment sentences into a subject-noun phrase and a predicate-verb phrase. And the reader must frequently do this without graphic signposts (e.g., commas) to mark a nanosecond pause. Figure 6–2 gives an example.

It's so much easier to interpret (and visualize) the message when words are effortlessly recognized *and* sensibly grouped together. Appropriate chunking of words into meaningful units facilitates the reader's ability to integrate another aspect of fluency—one that reveals personal interpretations. Allington (1983) connects fluency with *prosodic* reading.

It's About Prosody

Fluent reading can be characterized as *prosodic*. Efficient readers also use their knowledge of oral language's prosodic features to understand text (Vacca et al. 2003). "Prosody is a linguistic concept that refers to such features in oral reading as intonation, pitch, stress, pauses, and the duration placed on specific syllables" (214). When the reading is effectively prosodic, I can hear the reader constructing meaning as she goes along. "It is clear that the amount of correct expression indicates to a trained ear how much the reader comprehends the text" (Hudson, Lane, and Pullen 2005).

I look for a balance of these features that creates *expressive* reading—reading that shows meaning making. The National Assessment of Educational Progress (NAEP) describes it as expression marked by *naturalness* (Pinnell et al. 1995). Therefore, I don't expect to hear an audition for drama queen!

I'm sure you've experienced situations of prosodic harmony. Remembering these will supply exemplars for comparison. To understand prosody, recall an effective speaker you've heard. A speaker's use of prosodic elements affects listeners'

Read this sentence word by word.

The . . . tall . . . man . . . swiftly . . . grabbed . . . the . . . unaway . . . balloon.

It's difficult to grasp meaning. You're anxiously waiting for each next word, hoping that it'll help you make sense of what you have so far. It's like a game of charades—working with the smallest units, word by word, trying to grasp the whole.

Try reading the sentence with an attempt to chunk words.

The tall . . . man . . . swiftly . . . grabbed the . . . runaway balloon.

Understanding is still an effort. You're trying to merge semi-chunked bits together as you go along. That's extra and needless cognitive work that keeps you from thinking about overall meaning.

Now read it chunked this way.

The tall man / swiftly grabbed the runaway balloon.

Try it with a little addition. There's more to get in one breath, but it sounds natural when we do it that way.

The tall man / swiftly grabbed the runaway balloon as it flew upward.

When the words are recognized effortlessly and read accurately in meaningful units like this, understanding is seamless.

But, readers beware! Sometimes the writer's creative use of words trips us up as we apply this phrasing rule of thumb. We stop and reread because we're momentarily perplexed. Then we're rescued by our knowledge of multiple word meanings and associated syntactical changes; we unravel the confusion. Hudson, Lane, and Pullen (2005, 712) offer this sentence as an example.

The young man the jungle gym.

I started out reading a subject-noun phrase: The young man. I expected a verb phrase to follow, but instead I found another noun phrase: the jungle gym. I backtracked and quickly realized that *man* had another meaning here, and both *man* and *young* were performing syntactic functions that were different from my first assumption. In this sentence, *man* is a verb that begins the predicate-verb phrase. The initial subject-noun phrase ends with *young*. *Young* is a noun in this sentence; it's not an adjective describing *man*, as I first read it. Aha, I said; I get it! I was ready to reread the sentence with appropriate phrasing.

The young | man the jungle gym.

figure 6–2 Chunking Words into Meaningful Phrases

comprehension. When everything's in sync, the message is easily understood (Rasinski 2005). Such an orator's voice modulates with appropriate stress on words and phrases, placing emphasis in just the right spots. This helps you *get the point*. His intonation (pattern of voice pitch) expresses such elements as feeling, anticipation, statement of fact, and questions. Such speakers are easy to follow; we're tuned in and understand their message. Great orators aren't born that way. They've had great models and lots of opportunities to practice. So too have prosodic readers. But one might wonder why so much attention is placed on oral reading fluency when most of the reading that students do beyond the primary grades is silent and independent.

Oral Reading Versus Silent Reading

We place so much attention on oral reading because there *is* a connection; oral reading fluency impacts silent reading. Proficient readers hear a silent inner voice when reading to themselves—one that developed with their growth in oral reading fluency (Pinnell et al. 1995). Researchers found that students' scores on a fluency rubric measure were strongly correlated with their scores on the silent reading comprehension section of the National Assessment of Educational Progress test (Pinnell et al. 1995). With such evidence of fluency's importance, I set my instructional priorities.

I want to build readers' desire to become fluent and their belief that it can happen. To accomplish this, I need to first convince them of the relevance of fluency. Then I need to provide students with examplars of fluent reading, opportunities to practice, and feedback on their progress. I sensitively offer feedback, but it's always truthful and constructive. I also nudge the reader toward further development, or *feed forward*, when I believe she has the ability but not yet the courage to take the next step. To effectively feed forward and backward, I need to constantly gather data on readers' current level of fluency.

Assessing Fluency

What gets assessed gets taught. Teachers know that they need to teach the skills that are measured. Hopefully, the skills measured are meaningful ones and the tools used truly assess them. I want to be sure that what I assess is also what I value. Appreciating its critical role in comprehension, I pay close attention to individual student's level of fluency, including *all* of its elements. This means that I systematically observe and document each critical component that I've outlined in this chapter before I evaluate data and report conclusions (Hudson, Lane, and Pullen 2005). However, I need to be sure the information I've collected is trustworthy before I plan fluency instruction. I examine my fluency-measuring procedures for reliability and validity.

I expect fluency assessment tools to be *reliable*. That means I can count on them to provide me with consistent measures of readers' fluency. It also means that I have to consistently use tools so that differences are actually the result of students' fluency level and not differences in the way I followed procedures. But reliability will not guarantee validity.

My assessment tool also needs to be *valid*. That means it measures genuine elements of fluency (Rasinski 2005). I check that the measure is structured to capture data on everything that's significantly related to fluency. But there's one more thing I'm interested in.

Assessment measures typically report their reliability and validity, but they less often talk about *utility*. I'm left to figure out whether there's any instructional usefulness for the data (Hilliard 1989) that are collected. What's the point if there isn't?

I'm pragmatic. I want a reliable, valid measure that's easy to administer, score, and interpret, but I also want it to give me specific information that I can use right now. If it doesn't I would only use it when required to do so by policy makers. (Rasinski 2005). Whenever possible I would adapt it or not use it at all.

Figure 6–3 contains a rubric that includes all of the ingredients for fluency. I use it to assess students' current level of fluency. Then I'm ready to efficiently coach them to the next level. But there are steps that precede this assessment.

After I introduce students to the rubric, I invite them to collaboratively score my oral reading fluency. We discuss their conclusions thoroughly. Allington (1983) suggests that demonstrations are especially important because written texts don't graphically map the entire journey to prosodic reading. Most readers can use obvious graphic markers (e.g., punctuation), but many need to see how the expert reader decides when to use prosodic elements when signals are missing, "the modeling of fluent reading teaches children to use the unmarked prosodic features" (558). Next, I have my students extensively practice scoring each other. Gradually, they gain confidence and competence as they read, score, share, and discuss results. Students become mindfully aware of critical fluency indicators. Following these experiences, I begin to assess them individually and triangulate each student's score on the fluency rubric with other data.

			Word-Reading Accuracy	
Reading Behaviors Related to Fluency				
Score	Confidence	Flow/Pace of Reading		Prosody/Expression
4	The reader completed the reading in a relaxed manner, quickly repairing mistakes to maintain smoothness and accuracy.	Most of the reading was completed in meaningful phrases. The reader's *flow* (movement across the lines of print) appropriately slowed down before resuming normal pace as she problem solved words, used expression, processed interpretations, or applied other thinking strategies without halting or word-by-word speaking.	Word-reading accuracy was high. The reader self-corrected most miscues.	The reader attended to punctuation and other print cues to effectively make changes in voice pitch, intonation, and word/phrase emphasis. The reader consistently used appropriate expression that reflected a construction of meaning with the text.
3	The reader was mostly relaxed, although she became slightly flustered when making a mistake and showed some difficulty getting back on track.	Much of the reading was completed in meaningful phrases, but a few parts were choppy (word by word; inappropriate phrasing). Most of the time the reader's *flow* (movement across the lines of print) appropriately slowed down before resuming normal pace as she problem solved words, used expression, processed interpretations, or applied other thinking strategies. There was some halting or disjointed speech noted.	The reader made and left uncorrected a few miscues that did not interrupt meaning.	There was evidence of the reader's attention to punctuation and other print cues. The reader often made changes in voice pitch, intonation, and word/phrase emphasis in ways that created appropriate expression and reflected a construction of meaning.
2	The reader appeared a bit nervous and became flustered when making mistakes. Getting back on track was a struggle.	Much of the reading was completed in halting, disjointed, or word-by-word speaking. The reader's *flow* (movement across the lines of print) was inappropriately slowed down as she tried to problem solve words, use expression, process interpretations, or apply other thinking strategies with and without success.	The reader made and left uncorrected occasional errors that did interrupt meaning.	The reader attempted to make changes in voice pitch, intonation, and word/phrase emphasis based on punctuation and other print cues. Expressive reading was also attempted, but it did not appropriately match the text or reflect a logical construction of meaning. Much of the text was read in a monotone voice.

figure 6–3 Rubric for Evaluating Fluency and Flow

		Reading Behaviors Related to Fluency		
Score	Confidence	Flow/Pace of Reading	Word-Reading Accuracy	Prosody/Expression
1	The reader was obviously nervous to a point that concentration on the reading was impaired.	Most or all of the reading was completed in halting and word-by-word speaking, punctuated by long hesitations. The reader's *flow* (movement across the lines of print) came to notable stops as she tried to problem solve words, use expression, process interpretations, or apply other thinking strategies with and without success.	The reader frequently made and left uncorrected errors that did interrupt meaning.	The text was read in a monotone voice with little if any attention to punctuation or print cues. There were no attempts to add emphasis, adjust pitch and intonation, or use expression.
score in each column ⟶				

Student's average fluency score = _____ (add scores for each column and divide by 4)

Comments (Strengths and Weaknesses):

(Adapted from Fountas and Pinnell 1996, 2001; Indiana Department of Education 2005)

figure 6–3 Continued

Taken together, the student's percent of word-reading accuracy, his WCPM count, and his score on the fluency rubric reveal a great deal about his ability to successfully navigate the text I've asked him to read. I analyze each area, including the multidimensional rubric score, to determine what's going well and what we need to work on.

When it's not going well—when my struggling middle school readers are dysfluent—I need to identify the glitch and turn things around as soon as possible. Rasinski and his colleagues report that "the issue of reading fluency goes beyond the primary grades" (2005, 22). My continued attention to fluency—attention I balance with other identified needs—is especially important since a lack of fluency has been noted as an area of greatest impairment for struggling readers beyond primary grades (Rasinski and Padak 1998). But I don't want to be the only one concerned about fluency. If I want struggling students to be part of their own solution, I need to help them appreciate what increased fluency will do for them.

Stecker, Roser, and Martinez report, "Fluency has been shown to have a 'reciprocal relationship' with comprehension" (1998, 306). I want students to understand that improved fluency is not an end in itself; our work on fluency increases their comprehension. And understanding, in turn, facilitates fluency. "The issue of whether fluency is an outgrowth or a contributor to comprehension is unresolved. There is empirical evidence to support both positions" (Stecker, Roser, and Martinez 1998, 300).

I frequently assess students' fluency within the context of the resources they're using day by day to evaluate reading flow with a variety of genres, writing styles, and text density. But sometimes I also need to dig deeper. This might be when a reader is having difficulty with a particular element of fluency. For example, when accuracy is low, I analyze the nature of the reader's errors.

Miscues

Miscues (errors) in oral reading give me a view of the reader's understanding or lack thereof. Meaningful substitutions indicate that she's making sense even though particular words are misread. Uncorrected, nonsensical miscues usually interrupt comprehension; they also demonstrate that she's not paying attention or is unable to make sense of this text. It's critically important to examine these windows on students' thinking.

The next chapter discusses how to analyze miscues made during the oral reading segment of the MRR. I analyze these to determine their meaningfulness, syntactic acceptability, and letter-sound match with the text word.

CD Practice with Fluency

Listen again to the oral readings on the CD, focusing on the reader's fluency. Talk with a colleague about each reader's degree of fluency. Use the rubric as a guide for your conversation and evaluation.

7

Miscues

Goodman (1973) appropriately called students' errors in oral reading *miscues* because they indicate where the reader missed *cues* in the written text—embedded clues for word identification. Flurkey suggests that miscue analysis retunes our ears to hear errors not as mistakes, but as something more natural to the language process—"in its interpretation of reading as a language process, miscue analysis shows that 'mistakes' aren't really mistakes; they are merely phenomena that occur in most any act of reading" (1995, 11). Goodman spoke of miscues as "windows on the reading process" (1982, 93)—or windows on students' thinking. Davenport describes miscues as "an unexpected response during oral reading" (2002, 23). Miscues allow us to see the cues that readers are using effectively, those they're using but confusing, those they're not integrating with other cues, and those they're not using at all. Selectively drawing students' attention to their own miscues builds awareness of how and why they went offtrack, the importance of self-monitoring, strategies for self-correction, and efficient processes for word recognition (Davenport 2002).

Miscue analysis continues to be at the center of meaningful diagnosis of readers' growth. Goodman (1973) concluded that miscues should be analyzed categorically and interpreted in relationship with the child's recall of what he read. Taken together, miscue analysis and retelling offer a glimpse of the reader's overall ability to process text and its meaning (Davenport 2002; Shea 2000).

Goodman (1973) described three categories of cues—graphophonic, syntactic, and semantic. The table in Figure 7–1 describes each. For the purposes of MRRs, I

Cue System	Description
graphophonic or letter-sound (L-S)	*Graphophonic* knowledge relates to the letter (grapheme) sequences in words and their relationship to a corresponding speech sound (phoneme). Sometimes more than one letter is used to represent a speech sound (e.g., *ai* for long *a*). Proficient readers use their knowledge of letter-sound relationships and patterns in the language to recognize words fluidly and effortlessly. They use this knowledge in conjunction with other cues.
syntactic (S) or grammatical	*Syntactic* knowledge is associated with one's awareness of sentence grammar (language structures). Readers use it to predict what kind of word would *fit* or maintain the intended surface and deep structures in the sentence. Efficient readers instantly cross-check their syntactic expectations with graphophonic cues.
semantic or meaning (M)	*Semantic* cues are derived from meaning—the meaning of the other words in the sentence and surrounding sentences taken as a whole. Readers must be able to read most of the words in a sentence and create an understanding with them in order to use semantic cues to decode an unknown one. When the predicted word is semantically appropriate and also fits when cross-checked with the other cue systems, chances are good it's correct (i.e., it's the word in the text).

figure 7–1 Categories of Miscues (Goodman 1973)

code the perceived use of graphophonic cues as letter-sound appropriate (L-S). I refer to cues related to grammar as syntactic cues (S). I mark the use of semantic cues as meaning appropriate (M) (Shea 2000).

Several researchers have closely examined miscues and their relationship to students' level of reading proficiency with a piece of text (Clay 1991; Davenport 2002; Goodman 1973, 1982; Goodman, Watson, and Burke 1987; Goodman and Marek 1996). Their writing on the subject is extensive. Davenport's (2002) procedure, called over-the-shoulder (OTS) miscue analysis, entails a detailed recording and review of readers' miscues during oral reading and of the quality of their retelling. An OTS miscue analysis is intended for use with older readers—readers beyond the emergent stage who are more fluent, approaching fluency, or struggling to become fluent. Collected data on the oral reading and follow-up retelling are carefully analyzed in the OTS procedure. Similarly, the MRR process described in this book is intended for use with older readers because it's a better match with readers and assessment needs at that stage. Routman concludes that running records "are increasingly misused for older, fluent readers. Such use was never intended, is unnecessary, and is not a good use of student or teacher time" (2000, 113). Although MRRs differ somewhat from RRs and the OTS miscue analysis process, they also include the critically important component of miscue analysis.

This chapter focuses on my use of miscues as windows on students' thinking with particular texts used for MRRs. Earlier, you learned how to record miscues and count total errors. This chapter succinctly discusses how I categorize readers' miscues and look for patterns of cue use, cue integration, cue misuse, and nonuse of the cueing systems.

Analyzing Miscues

After working with the reader, I transfer the errors and self-corrections I've recorded on my copy of the text to the One-Minute Probe Tally Sheet (Figure 3–3). I circle Y or N to indicate whether or not insertions, omissions, or mispronunciations were meaningful. I acknowledge that this decision is subjective and based on the text. Then, one by one, I analyze the uncorrected substitutions made by the reader. I write Y for each cue system I assume the reader used (or attempted to use) as he made the miscue. Those I deem unused are noted with a dash (—).

Meaning-Appropriate Substitutions (M)

I place a Y in the M column if the substitution makes sense and doesn't interrupt the overall meaning of the sentence *and* the paragraph or passage. Sometimes miscues make sense in the immediate context, but not beyond. Meaning-appropriate substitutions may or may not reflect use of the other cueing systems. Consider the following sequence of sentences. The reader anticipates a new word at the end of the last sentence and begins to make predictions.

> The highway marked the western edge of the protected land. Campers used the wooded areas, streams, and fields within its boundaries. Many animals also made this their home. Deer lived in the . . .

While approaching the next word, a reader might predict *forest*, *fields*, or *woods* for the actual word that's there; it would depend on his schema for deer habitats and how well he's comprehended and integrated the text to that point. Let's say the text word is *preserve*. In the context of the sentence alone, each of the listed predictions would be meaning appropriate. However, in the broader context of the passage about a specific deer habitat in protected land, the substitutions don't fully relay the concept of this particular habitat. The reader who made such substitutions did not grasp the content-specific term that was introduced, but he did make a substitution that made sense and seems not to have severely interrupted meaning. The reader's retelling would reveal whether or not the substitution affected comprehension. Maybe the reader understood the concept, but just could not figure out the name for it.

There's often the most disagreement among evaluators (e.g., teachers) regarding semantic or meaning appropriateness. I generally try not to be too far-reaching or liberal, unless the reader clearly demonstrates that the substituted word has similar meaning for him. The following chart shows how I would code several samples miscues. I've filled in all three cue columns. I discuss syntactic and letter-sound appropriateness in the following two sections; after reading them, you can go back to this chart to see if you agree with my coding.

Reader Says	Text	Error Match		
		M	S	L-S
forest	preserve	—	Y	—
cars	automobiles	Y	Y	—
woods	forest	Y	Y	—
house	cottage	Y	Y	—

Syntactically Appropriate Substitutions (S)

Syntactically appropriate miscues fit in the grammatical structure of the sentence; the miscue matches the text word in part of speech, number (singular or plural), and/or tense (e.g., with verbs). Note the following examples with the caveat that the context of the text and the reader's retelling were factored into each decision.

Reader Says	Text	Error Match		
		M	S	L-S
grape	grain	—	Y	Y
gain	grain	—	—	Y
horse	horses	Y	—	Y
bigger	biggest	Y	—	Y
jumps	jumped	Y	—	Y
leaped	jumped	Y	Y	—

Again, the miscue may or may not be meaningfully appropriate when it's syntactically appropriate. I have to maintain a focus on the criteria when scoring miscues for the S category because it's so easy to be swayed when the miscue is meaningful. Instances of syntactic appropriateness (even without meaning) reveal a strong sense of language; the reader knows the kind of word that goes in that place because she's heard and used language to communicate. But even when the reader is maintaining grammatical structure, meaning may be confused. Some readers are aware that they're sacrificing meaning but proceed anyway. Proficient readers, on the other hand, aren't satisfied when their word identification attempts don't make sense. They stop when meaning is interrupted, go back to reread, and apply fix-up strategies.

When I ask readers, "It sounded like you read _____ right here. Did that make sense to you?" they typically respond with a shake of their head to say no. For example, if the reader said, "Deer live in the present," I'd score cue usage like this.

Reader Says	Text	Error Match		
		M	S	L-S
present	preserve	—	Y	Y

In the previous examples, there are a number of matches in letter-sound appropriateness. The L-S cueing system was used in attempts to decode these words but was not always used in harmony with other cueing systems.

Letter-Sound Appropriateness (L-S)

Letter-sound appropriateness refers to similarities between the miscue and the text word when analyzed independently for letter-sound matches. Sometimes the similarity is minimal. When it's only a beginning sound, I don't credit it with appropriateness in this category. When the match is more than that, I assume the reader used the L-S cueing system to some degree. I've also noticed that L-S-appropriate miscues often have a shape or length (configuration) similar to the text word.

Knowledge of phonics and word structure coupled with the ability to apply it on the run potentially increases readers' efficiency. However, when this knowledge is not balanced with information from other cue systems, its benefit wanes. Miscues that reflect overreliance on or a singular use of the L-S cueing system are typically significant; miscues that maintain meaning, even without attention to L-S cues, tend to be insignificant.

Significant and Insignificant Miscues

Miscues that interrupt meaning are *significant*; those that do not interrupt meaning are *insignificant*. A miscue that matches in all three categories of appropriateness would most likely be insignificant. However, the retelling must be factored into the final decision on miscue significance or lack thereof. Although I try to be as objective as humanly possible, I know that subjectivity enters into my decision as well as the decisions of others. That's why I've stopped making such a distinction when using RRs or MRRs for *benchmark assessments* or when using informal reading inventories where there's an option to factor in only significant miscues when calculating the percent of accuracy. Benchmark assessments are those that are used periodically to consider whether a student's performance meets established criteria or standards, where he fails on a continuum of expected growth, or to establish a level of performance at a point in time. Results are shared beyond the classroom and have importance on a schoolwide level. Accuracy scores on benchmark measures that don't factor in insignificant miscues tend to create inconsistent evaluations of students' competency from teacher to teacher in a school site. However, assessment is often done for reasons other than benchmarking. With different purposes, data are evaluated differently.

Less formal assessments of oral reading—those completed to monitor students' day-to-day performance with classroom materials and to plan instruction—may not factor in all insignificant miscues. Insignificant miscues that alter shades of meaning or disregard terminology that's important for the specific content are factored in while others are not. I do this because I've found that even with slight differences in meaning, insignificant miscues have the potential to obscure nuances of meaning, specific points, or the author's style of expression. When the reader's miscues "change the author's message, subtly or dramatically, he can become confused and misinterpret the author's point or draw a false conclusion" (Shea 2000, 101). Excessive insignificant miscues begin to add up to broader differences in meaning.

Decisions to count or not to count miscues deemed insignificant are made at the classroom level with regard to lesson objectives and expectations for learning as instructional outcomes. When the oral reading is a benchmark assessment (often completed by the reading specialist or resource teacher in middle school), all miscues count. I've found that making a clear schoolwide distinction of which miscues *count when* and *why* helps everyone on a team understand the assessment data they're reviewing in a case study. However, I add my conclusions about the reader's significant miscues to the team's discussion and suggest consideration of what we have collectively noticed.

Failure to draw attention to selected insignificant miscues—those that seem to only subtly affect understanding—perpetuates an attitude of indifference to the author's words and intention. It also fails to encourage self-initiated correcting of miscues.

Self-Corrected Miscues

The one-minute probe yields more than a score for the student's word-reading accuracy; it also provides a window into her comprehension. While that insight is not as thorough as evidence that comes from a retelling, it is important. Readers demonstrate understanding when they use appropriate expression and intonation while reading aloud. They also show they're thinking about meaning when they self-correct. "Self-corrections are reflections of a reader's comparing different sources of information, finding them discrepant, and doing something about correcting the discrepancy" (Johnston 1992, 86). The self-correcting reader recognizes when meaning is confused and seeks to regain understanding. This doesn't mean that all readers who are not verbally self-correcting lack understanding or fail to self-monitor. They may be silently rectifying miscues that interrupt meaning. Readers are more likely to incorporate the behavior in their oral *and* silent reading. If you want it to happen, identify self-correction behavior when it is observed and celebrate it with the reader.

I point out self-corrections in our postprobe discussions, complimenting the reader's self-monitoring and fix-up strategies. I make it clear that self-corrections improve comprehension and eliminate errors. I also point out that self-initiated repetitions, often used for self-correcting, don't count as errors. Purposefully used repetitions are good reading behaviors. Some readers believe they must move continuously forward through a text—without any recursive sidestepping—to be successful. The fact that I've recorded their self-corrections shows readers I'm interested in documenting their use of this fix-up strategy.

Miscue Patterns

The analysis of miscue patterns on a single MRR will be insufficient for drawing conclusions on cues used, cues integrated, and cues not used. You will need an array of miscues from several MRRs before a distinct pattern of cue usage will begin to emerge. However, there's a caveat I need to share here. When a student is reading frustrational-level text, miscue patterns reflect dependence on the L-S cue system, often with the exclusion of the other systems. That's because readers can't read enough of the text to engage meaning and syntactical cues. For older readers struggling with content area texts that are beyond their instructional level, this is often the case.

Struggling readers may be able to use meaning and syntactical cues with easier texts, but not with the texts you're expecting them to use in class. I keep this in mind as I use data from my miscue analysis in planning future lessons. When the required texts are at students' frustrational level, I have to plan ways to help them access information. But I also want to increase their skills in reading for information in my discipline. For this practice, I provide ancillary texts at students' instructional level—ones that reinforce the curricular content. I enlist the help of the school librarian and reading specialist in securing additional resources.

Although my primary focus is on curricular content, I plan interventions that simultaneouly build literacy competence. My differentiated instruction complements services provided by resource teachers (e.g., a reading specialist or a special education teacher). Miscue analysis helps me plan interventions that reinforce strengths in cue usage and emphasize the need for a balanced, well-orchestrated use of the three cueing systems. I add the findings from the miscue analysis to other MRR data.

Where Do I Go from Here?

Armed with MRR results, differentiated instructional methods, availability of ancillary resources, and support from resource staff, I feel ready to uncover glitches and meet the challenge of ameliorating them. But before I forge ahead and plan instructional remedies, I reflect on my understanding of the multifaceted aspects of comprehension. I have consciously made every effort to keep comprehension front and center throughout the assessment process. Now that focus directs my follow-up teaching. After all, comprehension is the always the bottom line.

The next chapter examines comprehension at the surface and deep levels, discussing what should happen at each level as the reader constructs meaning. An expectation of what should happen becomes my road map; it gives me markers to look for.

CD Practice—A Complete MRR

Follow along with the complete MRR model on the CD. Then, try to score a complete MRR on your own. Discuss your marking and scoring with a colleague.

8

On the Way to Comprehension

Comprehension Processes

I repeatedly emphasize to my students that the bottom line *is* comprehension. Without understanding, a text has not been read. The reader has simply said words and phrases. Remember the secret decoder ring? That's an analogy for full understanding of text.

Whenever I think of *decoding,* a memory of long ago comes to mind. I remember the secret decoder ring I waited so long to get. After saving Ovaltine labels and many allowances, I mailed in my order and eagerly anticipated the arrival of my package. I was confident that I'd be able to *break* secret codes with information in my decoder ring, just like real secret agents in the CIA. As soon as the postman brought it, I matched each coded symbol to its equivalent English letter, formed words and sentences, and *read* the messages. Once I had the secret message figured out, I knew it was *decoded* and I'd used the ring successfully. Not before. Although we find the term *decoding* used to describe word recognition, full decoding—just like figuring out a secret message—requires more than recognizing letters and words. It requires *getting* the message, just like decoders in the CIA. Full decoding or comprehension of the author's message is a complex process that happens behind the eyes—in the mind. Vision is a vehicle for gathering data the mind needs to make sense of the written message. Irwin (1991) suggests a model for understanding the complexity of comprehension. Out of necessity, the processes she defines are presented here one by one, but that is not meant to imply a hierarchy. They can happen in any order, in any combination, or simultaneously, depending on the characteristics of the reader and the text as well as the demands of the situation. When comprehension breaks down, it's because of glitches in one or more of these processes. We have to find and fix glitches through efficient diagnostic assessment and teaching. Our quality maintenance keeps readers well tuned as they motor along the road of literacy development.

Irwin's Model

Judith Irwin's (1991) model for the complex cognitive act of comprehension describes five processes that operate in a relatively simultaneous manner. Irwin's processes create an interactive model that "does not define flow as unidirectional" (Garner 1987, 2). Figure 8–1 outlines these comprehension processes. Although there's no hierarchy of importance, I describe the aspects here in an imposed order.

Five Aspects of Comprehension	
Micro Processes	Chunking words into meaningful phrases
Integrative Processes	Building connections between sentences and paragraphs
	Understanding word referents
	Making mini-inferences between sentences and paragraphs
Macro Processes	Getting the gist—organizing and summarizing
Elaborative Processes	Adding personally constructed meaning
	Creating mental images
	Responding affectively
	Making predictions
	Integrating prior knowledge
	Applying higher-level thinking
Metacognitive Processes	Monitoring one's understanding
	Self-initiating fix-up strategies

figure 8–1 Five Aspects of Comprehension (Irwin 1991)

INVESTIGATING MRR RESULTS

Micro Processes

First, there are the *micro* processes, which include word chunking (stringing together into meaningful phrases). The ability to read in natural phrases was discussed in Chapter 6 as a critical component of fluency. To string words together appropriately, the reader must have a basic understanding of the meaning conveyed by the words. For example, instead of reading words in a sentence separately, the reader chunks words into phrases that create units of meaning.

Word-by-Word-Reading

The . . . big . . . brown . . . bear . . . slept . . . soundly . . . in . . . his . . . cave . . . while . . . hibernating . . . all . . . winter.

Reading in Meaningful Phrases

The big brown bear / slept soundly in his cave while hibernating all winter.

Appropriate phrasing creates fluent reading and enhances understanding as words and sentences are strung together into meaningful units (orally or silently).

Integrative Processes

Next are the *integrative* processes, which require the reader to build connections by bridging sentences and paragraphs together, understand word referents, and make mini-inferences between sentences and paragraphs. For example, when the student reads the following in a text, he needs to immediately understand that *he* in the second sentence refers to the boy mentioned in the first sentence and *it* represents the new fishing pole. From prior knowledge he'll have to understand that the expression *catch of the day* means a fish. He'll also have to make the connection that the author is referring to the local pond in the first sentence with the phrase *in that spot* in the second sentence. Finally, the reader should predict that the boy caught a fish because he *concluded* that the new pole was a good investment.

> The boy tried out his new fishing pole in the local pond. He concluded that it was a good investment for getting the catch of the day in that spot.

Macro Processes

The third aspect is the *macro* processes, which involve getting the gist—the big idea or overall meaning. This is reflected in students' ability to effectively organize and summarize what they've heard or read. Cecil and Gipe (2003) emphasize that summarizing is different from retelling. They state that "in retelling the student tries to include as much as possible, whereas in a summary the goal is to be concise" (240). Tierney, Readence, and Dishner (1995) describe a procedure for building skills in summarizing succinctly. Students are guided step by step toward constructing a twenty-word gist statement for a passage they've read.

Elaborative Processes

The next aspect is the *elaborative* phase, in which students add their own voice and personally constructed meaning to the retelling as they share predictions, background knowledge, affective responses, and higher-level thinking. In this phase, the reader's schema on hibernation might cause her to visualize (when reading the earlier sentence) a fat bear—a bear that's spent time in the summer and fall building up the fat his body needs for functioning (even at a lowered metabolism) throughout winter's slumber.

Metacognitive Processes

Lastly, there's the *metacognitive* aspect, in which listeners or readers monitor their own understanding and apply fix-up strategies. They go back to reread or they ask for repeats of specific information that was unclear; they pose questions for clarification. Garner explains that metacognition relates to "learners' knowledge and use of their own cognitive resources" and reports that this "can help explain performance levels, and can offer a theoretical framework for devising instructional interventions to promote greater strategy use among readers" (1987, 1).

Some children become skilled with these processes in a natural way as they listen to others and begin to engage in reading on their own. Their early literacy experiences form a solid foundation for these aspects to evolve and grow.

Whole to Part and Back to Whole

From early on, children's universe is filled with the stories and essays that create the tapestries of their lives. They listen to narratives, expositions, and persuasions constructed by those around them to interact, explain, teach, comfort, or convince. Many children are also fortunate enough to hear written forms of these structures regularly read aloud. Children are enveloped with the wholeness of these stories and essays as they process meanings; they love to hear old favorites over and over.

Young children organize and summarize information in their own voices. As they do so, they begin to elaborate with personally constructed meanings that reflect higher-level thinking, affective responses, and predictions. They are constantly building intersentence connections (integrative) and repairing their own confusions (metacognitive); they ask questions when they don't understand. The incessant *why* becomes their heuristic tool. In these experiences children operate from a broad context since they aren't *performing* the text (orally or through reading) themselves. When children initially begin to perform the text, their focus changes.

Beginning readers focus their attention on the micro level. They're guided to recognize words, understand word meanings, chunk words into meaningful phrases, and read these phrases with appropriate expression and intonation. While children are mastering these micro processes, their attention to the other aspects may be temporarily diverted. Teachers support the other comprehension processes, sometimes carrying readers along while they're consumed with learning micro skills. Teachers do this to ensure that readers never forget that it's all about meaning. It's much like the poem about footprints in the sand. At this point, the teacher's footprints in the sand of broader comprehension processes may be the only set to be found. This temporary piggyback is important. It guarantees that comprehension is not overlooked while students are learning processes at the micro level. As readers acquire competence with micro processes, they ease back into taking responsibility for simultaneously using the other processes. Well-integrated use of all of these processes leads to a quality product—fully developed comprehension. However, when the processes fail to yield a fully formed product, discovering the missing ingredient becomes critical. We have to *autopsy* the reading act process by process to find glitches.

Active Engagement at the Global Level Before, During, and After Reading

Klinger and Vaughn (1999) describe a method they call *collaborative strategic reading* that combines comprehension strategy instruction with cooperative learning, engaging readers as active participants in reading. The method has defined before-, during-, and after-reading components that focus readers' attention on the process and product aspects of reading. As readers follow the steps, they seamlessly integrate Irwin's (1999) five processes. When phases of the collaborative strategic reading are completed orally, the teacher is able to gather evidence that pinpoints comprehension glitches.

Before Reading: Preview, Predict, and Set Purposes

Before reading, efficient readers survey the text in order to preview what the text will cover. Surveying "teaches students how to be selective about their reading, how to hone in on exactly the information they're interested in" (Routman 2003, 123). Students draw on their prior knowledge related to the topic and begin to predict information the text will reveal as well as questions they expect it will answer. These questions create real purposes for reading—purposes that are meaningful to the reader.

Preview ● Older readers preview the text before they read, much like younger readers take a *picture walk.* A picture walk involves spending a few minutes looking through pages of the text, attending to illustrations that activate and build a schema for the reading as well as anticipation for possible vocabulary that will be used by the author (Routman 2003). When previewing, older students skim the section they'll read, noticing headings and subheadings, charts, pictures, and other visual clues (Cecil and Gipe 2003; Manzo, Manzo, and Thomas 2005). Spending a few minutes previewing before plunging into the text prepares the way for efficient comprehension.

Readers use previewing to stimulate interest, pose questions they hope will be answered, activate their background knowledge, and make logical predictions about the text's content. Previewing time will vary based on the length of text. However, approximately eight minutes are recommended for readers to skim through the text, activate a schema on the topic, make logical predictions, and discuss ideas with others (Klinger and Vaughn 1999).

Predict ● Smith states that "prediction through meaningfulness is the basis for language comprehension" (1977, 388). Such prediction differs from random guessing. It involves "the elimination of unlikely alternatives on the basis of prior knowledge" (388). Logical predictions are constructed from the fabric of one's schema, but they're also constructed from readers' knowledge of the author's work and the structure of the literary genre. As they read, students check how closely their predictions match information in the text; they adjust working predictions and continue to construct new ones at appropriate junctures in the text (Tompkins 2003). Ongoing prediction setting, checking, and resetting establish purposes for reading. When integrated with personal wonderings, these purposes recursively propel readers through text as they work at making sense.

Set Purposes ● Purposes typically take the form of questions posed by the teacher, the reader, or both. Tompkins states, "The goal of teacher-directed purpose set-ting is to help students learn how to set personally relevant purposes" (2003, 35). Purposes set a course for readers, directing information selection and connection building. In setting purposes, readers activate their schema on the topic to discern what they already know, expect the text to substantiate, or hope to learn from the text. Readers also begin to anticipate which strategies will most efficiently lead to the accomplishment of their purposes (Tompkins 2003). A good mix of thick and thin questions establishes the most useful purposes for reading.

Thick questions call for making personal interpretations, engaging in critical or creative thinking, drawing conclusions, or building connections. Thin questions require answers that paraphrase information stated in the text (Harvey and Goud-vis 2000). Students' questions direct their attention toward finding answers and searching for information in the text; they respond to questions with facts, inter-pretations, and conclusions.

During Reading: Process Information

Influence of Personal Schema ● It's important to understand how prior knowl-edge, or lack thereof, influences students' interactions with text types and topics as they read. Garner (1987) explains that when new information is compatible with what we know, it's easily assimilated into our knowledge. The new information is accommodated; it expands and enriches our existing schema. "We can add pieces of information to an old schema . . . or we can modify an existing schema . . . or we can structure whole new schemata" (10). A reader with a rich schema on the topic might read globally or top down, compensating for weak decoding skills by effec-tively applying background knowledge for understanding. When such reading is silent and all we have is a measure of comprehension, it leaves the impression that the text's level was appropriate. However, it was simply the text's content that was comprehensible. Weak readers may also overcompensate with a schema by disre-garding what they can't or choose not to attend to in a text. The result is limited acquisition of new knowledge or limited correction of misinformation in their schema. Those skilled at decoding, but limited in their experiences, approach the task differently.

A reader who is skilled at decoding but lacks prior knowledge on the topic might strategically and temporarily attend closely to the word and phrase levels of a particular text, processing locally or from a bottom-up stance (van Dijk and

Kintsch 1983). After the initial processing, rereading gradually becomes global in nature since the reader has acquired background knowledge on the topic in the first reading. Skilled readers fluidly move back and forth in their reading stance (bottom up or top down) as they perceive the need to do so. This might be a conscious or unconscious perception.

The Between-Global-and-Local-Processing Cha-Cha ● Proficient readers adjust their stance from global to local fluidly to meet the demands of the text and their understanding. When reading relatively simple passages, texts for which we have a substantial schema, or genres with predictable structures, we're likely to rely on top-down processing. However, Garner suggests, "For technical prose, on the other hand, in which expectations and structural constraints are less pronounced, reliance on more bottom-up processing is usually appropriate" (1987, 3). By no means does this exclude active prediction setting and prediction checking while reading expository text, but it does shift the emphasis to what's on the page (Garner 1987). Too often, readers have not been taught how to adjust their reading behaviors or how to apply appropriate strategies when processing specific types of text. They're left to intuit refinement of general comprehension skills. Some readers do; some don't.

Personalized Strategy Tool Belt ● Harris and Sipay (1990) describe a particular strategy some readers use when processing text, called subvocalization. "Subvocalization is defined as 'silent speech' in which the mechanisms normally used in producing speech are activated but the words are not spoken or whispered" (1990, 643). However, they also suggest "visible signs of subvocalization may diminish, but it rarely, if ever, disappears entirely" (643). I can personally substantiate the last statement.

I've never been one who comfortably studies in libraries because it's hard for me to always remain quiet when studying. I did graduate work when my children were in elementary school. The family joke—a response to the mumbling in my bedroom (the only place for seclusion in our small house)—was "Mom's studying again!" Without thinking about it, I would move in and out of quiet and louder subvocalizing while processing dense required readings. However, I don't subvocalize when the text isn't dense, when I have adequate background knowledge on the topic, or when the stakes for interpreting the author's intent are not particularly high.

Harris and Sipay state that "many readers report hearing the words as if they were spoken by an inner voice. This phenomenon is similar to the inner speech that occurs in the mind during thinking and may be a similar process" (1990, 643–44).

Opinions about the usefulness of subvocalization vary widely. For obvious reasons, I agree with reported conclusions that it has the potential to aid comprehension when used effectively and discriminatingly (Harris and Sipay 1990). However, subvocalization isn't the only strategy I have on my comprehension tool belt when the going gets tough. It's one example, but it would never be enough for me or anyone else. Readers must have a working knowledge of several strategies, must be able to select the most appropriate one for a given situation, and must be able to self-initiate its use when understanding begins to clunk instead of click along (Klinger and Vaughn 1999).

Clicking and Clunking ● The *clicking* and *clunking* described by Klinger and Vaughn (1999) align with Irwin's metacognitive aspect of self-monitoring. While reading, students are clicking when they're aware that their understanding is full and complete. They've comprehended the gist, made various connections, and constructed personal meaning with the text. In other words, they've fluently processed the text and its content—gears were turning without any glitches—and they know it.

On the other hand, when understanding breaks down, clunking takes over. Students can learn how to recognize clunks, identify what causes them, and ameliorate problems. Keene and Zimmermann claim that many students "don't know when they're comprehending . . . [and] when they're not. They don't know whether it's critical for them to comprehend a given piece. And if they don't comprehend, they don't know what to do about it" (1997, 34). The interactions surrounding protocols for taking running records intensify students' ease with identifying and taking control of their own clicking and clunking while reading. After clicking through the text and repairing clunk-causing glitches, readers engage in closure activities.

After Reading: Wrap Up

Once the entire text has been read, students review its overall message and consider which of their questions were answered. The MRR procedure for putting this together in a concise manner provides structures that soon become internalized.

Although the procedure is somewhat standardized, retellings are not. They're customized to the text and meaning constructed by individual readers. At the same time, retellings are more and less than the text since the reader embellishes the content with personal connections, inferences, and reactions and also eliminates parts deemed nonessential to sharing the author's message (Garner 1987).

When comprehension reflected in this wrap-up is faulty or fragmented, we have to consider whether students are uncomfortable with retelling, lack an understanding of expectations for retelling, neglected to actively process the text as they decoded it, or had glitches that resulted from problems at the micro level.

Summary

In this chapter I discussed the components of comprehension—what should happen in each and where glitches might occur. Diagnosing the source of a glitch is a huge first step. Next, the question is What are you and the reader going to do about it? Without action that flows from a good answer to that question, the information becomes useless.

The next two chapters discuss glitches in different phases of the reading process and suggest ways to remediate them. Although not as exhaustive a list as found in any compendium, these chapters present effective, research-based strategies and practices to begin fixing glitches.

9

Repairing the Glitches at the Micro and Integrative Levels

Reading is communication—a conversation between an author and a reader. But the conversation is not spoken and the discussants are not together. To convey ideas, an author encodes them into a written form using print conventions relative to the particular language code he's using. To converse with authors, my students need to *decode* the message; they need to figure out the words that were encoded in the language. But they need to do much more than that.

Decoding at the word level isn't enough for comprehension, but comprehension isn't possible unless there's successful decoding at the word level. Students recognize this connection between knowing the words and understanding. Vacca and his colleagues report "Many students admit that sometimes they don't understand what they're reading because the words are too hard" (2003, 282).

Prior knowledge factors into the equation as well. An actively engaged schema on the topic facilitates decoding because preexisting knowledge helps students recognize words. Sometimes these are words they've heard but never seen in print. When the context is supportive, such words are easily recognized. Tom exclaims, "Oh, that's *pneumonia.* I never saw it before." At other times, new terms—ones never heard or seen before—are introduced in a text. If Tom has sufficient knowledge of phonetic and structural principles to pronounce them and the author has provided a rich context that reveals meaning, Tom will read and understand these words with minimal effort.

Recognizing Words and Chunking for Meaning

As words are decoded, their meaning must rapidly be understood. But words also need to be instantly strung together for comprehension at the sentence, paragraph, and passage levels. We already looked at this in connection with fluency. When reading is efficient, full decoding occurs seamlessly. Everything appears to happen at once—figuring out words, stringing them together, and understanding in large meaningful units. When the end result, understanding, breaks down, we work backward to target the problem. Then we work forward to ameliorate it.

This chapter will explore problems in word identification at the micro level and word stringing at the integrative level. The integrative level requires meaningful word chunking into phrases, understanding word referents (e.g., pronouns referring to nouns previously named), comprehending figures of speech, and meaningful chaining from sentence to sentence. Chaining (connecting) demands cross-checking and inferring as sentences are tied together. Irwin (1991) calls these *slot-filling inferences*. Let's look at how all of this fits together in the following paragraph.

> The man worked a long shift. His shoulders were slumped and he hung his head as he trudged along. When he got home, he took off his heavy coat and hung it in the closet. Then he slowly climbed the wooden stairs. Each seemed to creak loudly as his weight was placed on it. He wondered if his wife had already gone upstairs because she wasn't in the kitchen as usual when he got home. Then he remembered that she had been feeling a bit *under the weather* lately.

This is a short passage with relatively easy words, but understanding requires a lot of instant message decoding, connecting, and constructing.

After decoding each word automatically, I have to connect the word referents that litter this paragraph. Throughout the sentences, *he* and *his* refer us back to the man; *it* in the second sentence refers to the man's coat. *Each* and *it* in the fifth sentence refer to individual steps—a different reference for this *it*. *She* in the fifth sentence refers to the man's wife. I also need to understand that *hung his head* isn't meant to be taken literally; it means that the man's head was falling forward and leaning downward as when someone is very sleepy. I also need to be familiar with the expression *under the weather*, used here to suggest that his wife was ill. The slot-filling inference I made was that the man was tired because he'd worked a long shift. The description of him trudging along with his head down reinforces my inference. I also predicted that when he got upstairs he'd find his wife in bed because she was sick. I expected that he'd be going to bed since he was so tired.

These associations came automatically and effortlessly as a result of recognizing words, appropriately stringing them together, thinking about meaning, and making inferences.

Over and over, I emphasize to students that reading the words is necessary, but not enough. It's just the same with oral conversation. Hearing is insufficient. If we're just hearing—a physical reaction in our eardrums and brain—the words begin to sound like a droning noise. To comprehend, we have to *listen* to spoken words. Listening involves thinking about the integrated word strings and then the speaker's whole message. Word integration is critical—and sometimes that just doesn't happen. It seems incredible that readers can march through text with a high percent of accuracy and be clueless about what they've read, but it happens a lot!

Let's consider the initial text navigation steps of word identification and word integration in a communication between an author and reader. Keep in mind that they're not the only steps and they're not the most important steps. Strategies presented in this chapter target glitches in these areas. However, what's here is only a sample of an extensive array of possibilities found in texts devoted to the subject. When deciding on an instructional intervention, I look at ones that are research based. I might even do my own research with my adaptation of a research-based strategy. The instructional intervention I choose must have a good fit with the student and her specific area of need. I also like strategies that stimulate discussion—talk that spreads the wings of our thinking and meaning to an expanse we never expected to reach. Conversation "is the thread that is woven throughout the comprehension quilt" (Ketch 2005, 9).

Instructional Caveat

I have an instructional caveat I feel compelled to mention. My comments at this point foreshadow what I expand on in Chapter 11 when talking about implementing strategy instruction. The caveat is this: Remember the *real* purpose of strategy instruction.

It's too easy for students (and myself) to get caught up in procedural aspects of strategies. Sometimes students compulsively attend to the parts and pieces of good strategies, worrying about a next step and whether they did it just right. I've sometimes noticed robotic role playing and turn taking when students are working with a collaborative strategy. Sometimes even strategic writing—writing that's meant to help readers reflect and organize ideas for discussion—becomes formulaic and just another chore.

I want students to see strategies as paths to comprehension, not ends in themselves. I choose strategies that stimulate independent thinking and lots of discourse. The steps of strategies (including writing steps) are tools that spark the conversation and keep essential talk moving. Our discourse helps us affirm, refine, and expand on the personal meaning we've constructed with and across texts. "Hearing ideas discussed orally from another's point of view increases understanding, memory, and monitoring of one's own thinking . . . The oral process helps students clarify and solidify their thoughts" (Ketch 2005, 10).

With this said, let's move on to consider what to do when we pinpoint glitches in specific areas.

Planning Interventions: Matching Instruction to Needs

I'm able to implement successful instructional interventions that fix glitches only after I scrutinize students' MRR results, investigate their past academic histories (what's been tried before under what circumstances), do a survey of their interests, and determine what motivates them. But more importantly and before doing all that, I need to gain students' trust that my intention is to help them. I also need to empower them to realize that, by extending their own effort, they will steadily improve. A plan for each student is individually crafted but often executed in groups or with the whole class. Once in a while I get to work with students individually, but that's rare. More often I have to teach to the individuals within small groups or the entire class, applying what I know they need while I manage the group. It's a tough balancing act. I compare it to a juggler spinning several plates in the air at once, jumping from plate to plate as each begins to wobble. But teachers do this all the time; it's the mix of art and science in teaching at its best!

Prior Word Knowledge or Word Schemata

The micro level involves word recognition—the ability to accurately articulate the words and ascribe meaning to them. To do this, the reader must bring a repertoire of known words to the text. Word knowledge in a language is a critical ingredient for reading proficiency. Words label objects, concepts, and ideas. One must know the words before he can string them together meaningfully. This also includes familiarity with cultural language patterns and expressions of speech. Efficient word recognition requires a constantly evolving knowledge of words, their meanings, and the multiple, varied, and creative contexts in which they can be used. Nagy and Scott state that "knowing a word means being able to do things with it; to recognize it in connected speech or in print, to access its meaning, to pronounce it—and to be able to do these things within a fraction of a second" (2000, 273). Why, you ask, is there such a discrepancy in the depth and breadth of students' schemata for word recognition?

Research has identified key factors that distinguish children with large vocabularies from those with smaller ones. One factor related to levels of word learning is the amount of exposure students have to new words (e.g., in free reading, in conversations). Another is the extent to which adults (or competent peers) involve students in analytical discussions focused on word structure, derivation, and/or meaning (Snow 1993). Effective discussion about words (word study)—discussion that makes a significant deposit in a student's word bank (lexicon)—is ongoing across the day, both inside and outside of school.

In other words, those words that are first *in the ears and on the lips* will more likely be smoothly recognized when met in print. The depth and breadth of students' lexica influence their reading fluency and text comprehension. Researchers describe four stages of word knowledge:

1. The student has never heard or seen the word (unknown).

2. The student has heard the word or seen it before, but he doesn't know what it means (acquainted, but unknown).

3. The student recognizes the word's meaning based on its use in a particular context (acquainted).

4. The student knows the word. (Cecil and Gipe 2003; Beck, McCaslin, and McKeown 1980)

I adjust my plans for vocabulary instruction based on students' current level of word knowledge and how well they can access it.

I want students to understand that we access word knowledge whenever we're communicating, either orally or in print. We retrieve known words from our memory whenever we're thinking, talking, listening, and reading. Just and Carpenter (1984) concluded from their research that recognition of uncommon words takes longer and may cause confusion. This seemingly commonsense bit of knowledge is my rationale for preteaching new terminology or words students might not be familiar with before they read a text. I also continuously reinforce known words (e.g., those students have heard and used, but not read before) with brief, casual discussion that introduces a text and sets a purpose for reading.

I've found that multiple meaningful exposures, accompanied by conversation, help my students read new words fluently, understand them, internalize them, and use them appropriately in speech. This takes time and strategic planning. Hopefully, the nature of our discussion brings out meanings the word might have in immediate contexts as well as creative or culturally specific uses.

Dickinson and Tabors (2002) point out that extended discourse about new words provides information beyond that which is available in the context of a situation or printed text. However, for that to be accomplished, I need to ensure that word conversations are genuinely *dialogic* in nature. This is different from *recitation* that's highly didactic and oriented toward single right answers. When I weave vocabulary instruction into *word study*, I provide opportunities for grand conversations and collaborative examinations of words on many levels.

Word studies in our class spark students' curiosity about language—a curiosity that makes learning about words interesting rather than dreadfully boring. We analyze words for structure, form, and meaning within the immediate context. Sometimes our conversations get into the word's history, derivation, multiple meanings, and popular uses.

Imagine that—probative, interesting discussions about words! The suggestions that follow focus on building word schemata through word study that has talk at its core.

If . . . Then Scenarios for Problems at the Micro Level

I know that my students' vocabulary knowledge increases when they analytically discuss new words and when they're guided to make connections with personal concepts and word schemata (Dickinson and Smith 1994). These activities help students begin to *own* new words. That's my instructional goal for vocabulary teaching—transfer of word ownership. If MRR results reflect difficulty with word recognition, I recommend the following interventions for the *then* part of the problem-solution scenario. Each strategy includes attention to structure and meaning; each leads to student control.

Text Walk and Talk

In primary grades it's called a *picture walk*. With older students it's a *text walk and talk*. But picture walking and text walking and talking are simply teacher-guided versions of the skim and question steps (the S and Q) of Robinson's (1961) SQ3R (survey, question, read, recite, review) method, which is outlined in the next chapter. In the text walk and talk, I direct students through a cursory examination of the text's title, subtitles, illustrations, captions, charts, maps, legends, and other text aids provided by the author and invite them to talk about what they find. Our talk initiates comments, reactions, questions, and predictions; it also strategically marinates readers in the language of the text. In the process, key words and new words are *in the ears and on the lips* before students read them. These grand conversations, filled with rich language, deep thinking, and idea sharing, are the first and foremost way my students increase their automatic recognition of words.

Recently, before I had a seventh grader read "Rebirth of a City," by Jason Urbanus, we did a text walk that sparked a brief discussion about the Mount Saint Helens eruption a few decades ago as well as its more recent widely covered threat of eruption. This student had discussed the recent situation at home with her parents, who explained the event in the 1980s. Her schema on volcanic activity had recently been expanded. Our reading of captions on the page tied that schema to the eruption in Pompeii and introduced the words *Pompeii, Pompeians, eruption,* and *charred*. She subsequently read each of these words effortlessly and used them appropriately in her retelling.

In that instance, my job was made easier; Sidney's parents had already laid lots of schematic groundwork on the topic. When that's not the case, I lay a fine layer of schema and language during the text walk and talk—enough to scaffold students' first reading. The talking in this initial walking is comfortable and natural; it's also genuinely dialogic—neither teacher nor student is in control. It takes only a few minutes, but the time spent pays exponentially in dividends. My fine layer of word preparation also includes a closer look at selected words that I've decided need additional explanation and examination.

Examining Words in Word Study

I discriminately select words for vocabulary instruction before reading. I choose ones that I assume are new, unknown, and/or not highly supported with contextual clues. That means that I need to know my students well to effectively predict which words will present problems. I know that students whose experiences have not given them support in vocabulary acquisition are the most in need of rich conversations about words (Nagy and Scott 2000), but I don't want to spend time on unnecessary vocabulary instruction. I want to make my teaching efficient and differentiated so that I'm teaching "particular words to particular students for a particular purpose" (Blachowitz and Fisher 2000, 517). I keep my list of words for prereading instruction to a minimum. I also want to be sure that instructional activities I plan for these words

- link new words to students' experiences,
- elaborate on the meaning provided in the text,
- clarify word meaning with examples,
- stimulate discussion and questioning related to the word,
- lead students to determine categories for words, and
- draw students' attention to *distinguishing features* (structural elements) of words. (Cecil and Gipe 2003; Kibby 2004)

Words that I suspect will be *caught*—easily decoded with the support of rich clues in the context—are not directly *taught* before students read. This gives my students an authentic opportunity to use context clues to figure out words on their own. After each part of the reading, I bring up taught and untaught words in discussion of the text's content to be sure the student has understood them.

If the student didn't catch a word, I teach her the word in a more direct manner after reading. Thus, word study occurs before as well as after reading.

I consistently and consciously refer to our word discussions as word study because the term allows me to group seemingly disparate areas of instruction into one category. These traditionally disparate areas of instruction are phonics, spelling, and vocabulary. I never understood how or why I should schedule them separately. They always ended up overlapping; when we were doing spelling, it sometimes seemed like a phonics or vocabulary lesson. Word study takes a holistic approach—examining a word's structure, derivation, etymology, letter patterns, similarities to other words, letter-sound relationships, syntactical purposes, and variety of meanings.

The analysis of words from many angles does more than stimulate curiosity. It causes students to notice interesting, different, and precise words—or just words that have an appealing sound or interesting appearance. Curiosity also increases students' motivation to know and own words. Owned words are used effectively in speech and writing; known words are read fluently. The activities I choose to use during word study must support the kind of discussions and goals I've described.

Sorting Words

During a word sort, students sort words into categories. The words include content-specific terms or general utility words you're introducing to increase students' meaning vocabulary one notch at a time (Cecil and Gipe 2003). When done in small groups, word sorts provide students with opportunities for discussion that involves structural or meaning analysis. Use words that have previously been introduced or that you assume are already in students' lexica. You can give students a list of words and ask them to sort the words into predefined categories; this is a *closed sort*. Or you can give students the option of creating their own categories; this is an *open sort*. I allow students to have a miscellaneous category in an open sort because words will always be left over when they've named the categories. But the miscellaneous category cannot be larger than the other ones. If it is, they must come up with another category that will absorb words in the miscellaneous pile. You can never predict how this activity will come out, but the outcomes never cease to amaze me (Bear et al. 2000).

Students always come up with unexpected categories. There's also an abundance of word talk whenever sorting is going on. I like to have group members record their categories and the words under each on chart paper. There are further discussions and even challenges as groups share their different perspectives on the same group of words. Excitement about words is contagious; it becomes the driving force for word learning that increases fluency. When the sorts are completed, don't discard the word charts. You can bind the charts and make them available for student use or review. You can also place word cards on a class word wall.

Word Walls in the Intermediate Grades?

In a single word, yes! According to Cecil and Gipe, "Word walls are charts or bulletin boards on which important vocabulary words are placed, usually alphabetically, to be referred to during word study activities" (2003, 73). This definition fits what I call my general word wall. But I simultaneously have a smaller, categorical word wall that's associated with the topic of our current unit of study. Whenever a unit's completed, I add these words to the alphabetical word wall and change the smaller word wall's category to fit the next unit.

Word walls allow me to easily draw students' attention to particular words for quick reference or review. I often notice students looking at the word walls to find words for their writing or to just read them. It's important to remember that words placed on both word walls (alphabetical and topical) have been thoroughly analyzed for structure and meaning before they're added. To initiate discussions on their meaning, I always present words within a rich context.

Words in Context

I always present the words I've decided to teach—whether before or after reading—in context because I know students won't really learn words if I provide only abstract definitions. "It takes more than definitional knowledge to know a word, and we have to know words in order to identify them in multiple readings and listening contexts and use them in our speaking and writing" (Allen 1999, 8).

I try to use the exact context in which a word is found in the reading to model how I'd recognize the word and figure out its meaning. However, too often the context surrounding target words (the *natural context*) offers limited information (Nagy 2004). When that's the case, I also provide several original sentences that use the word in different ways. I model using the richer context in my sentences to figure out the word's meaning in each. After lots of discussion about the examples, students decide which use matches the purpose of the current reading. My additional sentences provide what Nagy (2004) calls *instructional contexts*. My instruction combines context and definitions. Nagy suggests, "A combination of definitional and contextual approaches is more effective than either approach in isolation" (8). The combination also increases reading comprehension (Stahl and Fairbanks 1986).

Nagy (2004) concludes that methods of *intensive vocabulary instruction* most effectively improve students' comprehension. These go even beyond the mere combination of context and definitions to focus on integration, repetition, and meaningful use.

I help students integrate new words with prior knowledge to ensure that each word is internalized and finds its place in students' lexica. Brainstorming activities, semantic mapping and webbing, word sorts, semantic feature analyses, Venn diagrams, hierarchical arrays, and linear arrays are but a few of the many activities that guide integrative thinking. But it's the sharing of integrative thinking that makes these activities effective—the talk generates learning!

I depend on activities that have students working collaboratively and ones that stimulate lots of discussion. But I also want students to know what they can do on their own, especially when the context is uninformative and a word is a stranger. I explain that sometimes readers have only the uninformative natural context to work with until they can seek other sources of information (e.g., other texts, dictionaries, glossaries, and other people). Often, until they can access such resources, readers move on with partial word knowledge, a bit of uncertainty, and occasionally confused concepts. They read on, assuming upcoming paragraphs in the text will illuminate what's currently confusing (Beck, McKeown, and McCaslin, 1980). I provide demonstrations of how this works with texts we're using. Students gradually begin to develop self-sustaining vocabulary problem-solving strategies.

Those students whose experiences have not given them support in vocabulary acquisition are the most in need of these vocabulary strategies as well as rich conversations about words (Nagy and Scott 2000).

Wide Reading Increases Vocabulary

"The more that you read, the more things [including words] you will know. The more that you learn the more places you'll go" (Seuss 1978, 27).

Students learn new words incidentally inside and outside of school all the time. They learn words and build background knowledge as they interact with parents, friends, and peers; background knowledge helps them use context to recognize and understand words quickly. But students also increase their vocabularies and build schemata on a wide range of topics through the free reading they do. Much has been written about the power of wide reading in increasing one's sight vocabulary, word knowledge, and background knowledge (Nagy, Anderson, and Herman 1987; Nagy, Herman, and Anderson 1985; Tompkins 2004; Pikulski and Chard 2005). "Children not only learn how to negotiate the meaning of new words and discover additional meanings for familiar words in different contexts, they also learn the importance of relating life experiences to literature" (Friedberg and Strong 1989, 41).

The amount of independent self-selected reading that a student engages in is the best predictor of his vocabulary growth between grades 2 and 5 (Fielding, Wilson, and Anderson 1986). Beyond third grade, independent reading is students' largest resource for word learning (Beck and McKeown 1991; Nagy 2004). Rycik and Irvin believe that "when students read extensively from books they have chosen, they have opportunities to encounter developmentally appropriate words and to see those words in a meaningful context in which they are most likely to stick" (2005, 168).

Researchers have shown that readers can also increase word and background knowledge when they listen to teachers read aloud. Actually, the increase can be as much as when reading independently (Stahl, Richek, and Vandevier 1991). Middle school students are not too old to enjoy and benefit from listening to the teacher read aloud. This is especially important for struggling readers, who typically do not do as much self-selected reading.

When I make highly motivating resources—ones matched to students' reading levels and interests—readily available, students are more likely to read independently. Reading and rereading high-interest, appropriate-level texts increases students' sight vocabulary, fluency, comprehension, and confidence. It's simple. Teaching is a lot like fishing: success is all about the choice and presentation of bait!

I make sure that I have a wealth of ancillary books, magazines, Internet sources, newspapers, and other real-world materials available for self-selected free reading related to current topics of study. Students frequently add what they've learned from other sources to the discussions we have about information from the textbook. They also ask questions about their supplementary readings when they don't understand something. We reread, looking closer for the source of confusion. Often, confusion reigns when ideas weren't integrated at the word, phrase, or sentence level.

If . . . Then Scenarios at the Integrative Level

As students read, they need to think in the present (where they are in the text), in the past (what they've learned so far in this text and elsewhere), and in the future (what they predict they'll learn in this text and what they want to learn). All of that happens instantly when processes at the integrative level are humming.

The paragraph about the tired man near the beginning of this chapter demonstrated that words, phrases, and sentences can't be read as isolated islands unto themselves. To understand, the reader must connect phrases and sentences within the text to each other and then fold that mixture into personal schemata. This is a complex cognitive process that requires active reading accompanied by thinking, questioning, wondering, cross-referencing, evaluating, and on and on. Some students don't understand that this is the reader's job or don't know how to do it. In such cases, I have to demystify the cognitive processes; I make them overt, observable.

I *chew and digest* selected complicated sections of texts in front of students. I read aloud and think aloud. I give them advanced warning that I will interrupt my reading by talking to myself. I don't want them to worry about seemingly peculiar behavior! I tell them that I want them to notice what I'm doing, saying, thinking, and wondering. We talk about this a lot!

The next step involves mediated support with students' thinking aloud. At this point, we work collaboratively to do a *close reading* (Tompkins 2001). To start a close reading, I read a difficult section of text aloud and stop to ask questions. Then students' respond. Their comments indicate how well they're integrating information and making connections. We work together to blaze a trail through the underbrush of dense text. I do a close reading for parts of texts that are particularly difficult, confusing, or fraught with entanglements that must be unraveled. Figure 9–1 shows an example of a close reading with a piece of literature; the close reading procedure is adapted from Tomkins (2001).

I've discovered that such demonstration of close reading and discussion that teases out the meaning is the most effective and efficient combination for teaching integrative-level skills.

The following passage comes from *Number the Stars*, by Lois Lowry (1989).

In this story the Johansen family is hiding Ellen, a Jewish girl, from the Nazis. They have established the ruse that Ellen is their daughter but still fear that the lie might be detected before Ellen can be brought to safety.

If students aren't integrating several clues in these few lines, they've missed critical details. They're also ill prepared for the events that unfold in the story. This section is at the beginning of Chapter 5.

Who Is the Dark Haired One?
"Do you really think anyone will come?" Ellen asked nervously, turning to Annemarie in the bedroom. "Your father doesn't think so."

"Of course not. They're always threatening stuff. They just like to scare people." Annemarie took her nightgown from the hook in the closet.

"Anyway, if they did, it would give me a chance to practice acting." (39)

This is how I might do a close reading of these sentences, integrating information with students as we go along.

Teacher reads aloud (TRA): "Do you really think anyone will come?" Ellen asked nervously, turning to Annemarie in the bedroom.

Teacher initiates discussion (TID) to stimulate the kind of thinking readers should spontaneously and concurrently do as they read: Who's the "anyone" that might be coming? Why would they be coming? Why is Ellen nervous?

TRA: "Your father doesn't think so."
TID: What does Annemarie's father think won't happen? Why does he think that? Why does Ellen think he's not concerned about it?
TRA: "Of course not. They're always threatening stuff. They just like to scare people."
TID: Who's always threatening stuff? Why? What stuff? Why do they try to scare people? Were they just scaring people, or were they really doing stuff?
TRA: "Anyway, if they did, it would give me a chance to practice acting."
TID: What does Ellen mean by practicing acting? Is she being silly or serious? What does acting have to do with who might be coming?

---

figure 9–1 Close Reading Example

Summary

This chapter examined comprehension at the word and integrative levels. Although much attention is given to what's on the page—literal information—at these levels, they are hardly confined to that. To decode words and integrate information, the reader needs to apply background information in making inferences, predictions, and connections.

The next chapter examines deep comprehension at the macro, elaborative, and metacognitive levels. Readers move between and beyond the words and sentences on the page, digging deep to build a strong foundation for their tower of personally constructed meaning.

10

Repairing Glitches in Global Meaning Processing

If reading is about mind journeys, teaching reading is about
outfitting the travelers, modeling how to use the map,
demonstrating the key and the legend, supporting the travelers as
they lose their way and take circuitous routes, until, ultimately, it's
the child and the map together and they are off on their own.
—Ellin Keene and Susan Zimmermann, *Mosaic of Thought*

To understand at a deep level, readers need to think about the text and make multilayered connections (Harvey and Goudvis 2000; Tompkins 2003). To assess and guide these processes, I ask students to *download* (verbalize) their thinking at strategic points in the reading; I want to examine with them the understandings they've constructed. I also want all of us to have an opportunity to consider each other's insights. "By discussing [a text], it's like we decided what it meant together" (Keene and Zimmermann 1997, 32). We build our meaning with conversation as the inspiration for design and the mortar that makes it solid. I know that talk "deepens our understanding of virtually everything we read" (7).

Students weave richer interpretations when they mingle ideas (whole or partial) they've heard with their own. In any classroom of diversity, shared perceptions—perceptions viewed from a lens shaded with the colors of cultural, social, and familial influences—bring many views of a point to the floor. "Different children bring different ways of constructing the world as a result of the cultures they grow up in" (Delpit 1991, 543). Probing unique insights opens up a world of possibilities, a world of connections, a world of empathy, a world of oneness. Sadly, much instruction diminishes voices in exchange for efficiency, uniformity, and streamlined curriculum delivery.

The kind of comprehension instruction that isn't focused on students' thinking—the kind centered on interrogation and convergence on a single right answer—doesn't create proficient, independent, confident, and critical readers (Keene and Zimmermann 1997). That kind of instruction creates students who mindlessly fulfill obligations for rewards or simply pass through school on their way to life.

One of my goals is to build a community of learners who are fully engaged in the here and now with their association of peers, teachers, and topics of study. I also want students to *think*—critically, creatively, and independently. Keene and Zimmermann state, "Teaching reading comprehension is mostly about teaching thinking" (47). My approach is threefold and cyclical. I plan teaching episodes (direct instruction) when necessary. Then, I guide on the side much of the time while students practice. Finally, I research what's working by observing and assessing my students' performances. Then it's back to teaching what they need.

I know I've been effective when I become progressively unnecessary—when my students have developed the self-sustaining strategies that define a literate, capable, and active learner at their developmental level. To accomplish this goal I must teach in a way that puts students in control of their own learning. When I focus on comprehension strategies that promote the personal construction of meaning and the open sharing of ideas, I've taken a step in the right direction.

This chapter examines glitches in comprehension, particularly where they occur and what can be done to effectively repair them and get readers moving forward. What's here is the tip of the iceberg. There are many compendiums of useful, research-based comprehension strategies, offering step-by-step guides for implementation (Fisher and Frey 2004; Harvey and Goudvis 2000; Tankersley 2005; Tierney, Readence, and Dishner 1995; Wilhelm 2001). It's important to note that strategy instruction and practice are not ends in themselves. My goal is for students to apply strategies on their own in a way that reflects logical integration and adaptation of procedures. I want students to *use* strategy tools—to eventually internalize and apply them in their own way to get at meaning.

In this chapter I describe strategies that have worked best with my students, particularly ones that incorporate multiple substrategies in their steps. You'll notice that conversation is at the heart of each. As the facilitator, I'm responsible for ensuring that all the talk and questions (students' and my own) in my classroom are "highly systematic, creative, and intensive" (Pogrow 2005, 65).

Helping Readers Construct Deeper Meaning

I want students to know they must dig for deeper meaning; it's not collected from the surface of the page. The essential ingredient for constructing deeper meaning is the reader's own thinking. I tell students that I can help. I can guide them, but I can't do their thinking. To get inside a text—to reach deep levels of meaning—my students must retrieve personal schemata, blend them with the author's ideas, and create a unique understanding. The sum of this activity, reading, is a "complex, recursive process" (Tovani 2000, 17) that operates on multiple levels. It involves a mix of aesthetic (feeling and emotion) and efferent (focused on information) responding. The reader decides his measure of each (Rosenblatt 1978).

Deep questions demand multilayered thinking; there's no one right answer. However, responses should be logical and grounded in the text and one's experience (Calkins 2001). Putting all that together can be overwhelming, especially when what you're supposed to do is a mystery—when you've never seen how successful readers do it. That's why I make the activity in my head visible for students; I think out loud, pulling aside the curtain to show the wizard—comprehension strategies in action (Tankersley 2005).

"We were convinced that reading comprehension could be taught by showing children what proficient readers thought about as they read and teaching children to use those same strategies themselves" (Keene and Zimmermann 1997, 24). I read aloud to my students. Yes, even middle school students like to sit back and enjoy good surround-sound literature (Tankersley 2005). I get lots of mileage from this activity that students consider chill-out time. How little they know!

- I'm building their background knowledge for the unit we're studying and lots more.
- I'm hooking them on reading.
- I'm presenting topics through many genres, demonstrating the forms and richness of literature.
- I'm marinating them in new vocabulary.
- I'm modeling decoding, fluent reading, and what I do when I don't understand.
- I'm using the strategies I want them to use.

As I read aloud, I think out loud. To help them understand "understanding," I let them see how I build it. I make sure to reread when I'm confused, demonstrating how useful a simple step can be. Routman reports, "Research consistently shows that rereading is one of the most highly recommended strategies for struggling readers. Yet, we rarely teach rereading as a primary strategy" (2003, 122).

I say to my students, "Let me show you what I do to figure out what I'm reading. You'll hear the gears clicking and clunking in my head while I think, because I'm going to talk out what's on my mind. It might seem kind of sloppy, but thinking doesn't have to be neat."

I work hard to make the transition from reading aloud to thinking aloud very subtle. Students can concentrate on listening and absorbing what they hear and observe while I'm reading. When I finish, I ask them to tell me what they saw. We build a list of the strategies they watched me use. I usually have to help them express their thoughts with clarity. But I never put words in their mouths. If they didn't see a strategy, my demonstration wasn't clear. I emphasize the strategy in subsequent readings. We continue until we've constructed a reasonable list. This takes time, but it's worth it. Students understand what they can identify; they begin to realize that good readers think along (turn the verbalizing inward) as they read, using the strategies on the list. Figure 10–1 shows a list of think-along strategies. However, once students understand how to think along, we don't totally abandon thinking aloud.

I frequently ask students to download their thinking when we start discussing what was read. This is an open-ended invitation that always spawns fascinating conversations. We also refer back to the chart to determine which strategies we

---

1. I look over what I'm going to read—the titles, subtitles, pictures, and captions.
2. I make predictions. I ask myself questions.
3. I check predictions, make new predictions, and try to answer my own questions.
4. I try to remember what I read. I stop, think about it, and retell a part. Sometimes I summarize with a gist statement.
5. I make pictures in my mind when there's a description.
6. I make brief comments that express my reactions.
7. I make connections with other texts, with my experiences, with the world.
8. I figure out the meanings of words using context clues.
9. I make inferences by mixing what's on the page with my experiences and what I know.
10. I evaluate the information and the author's writing.

figure 10–1 Think-Along Strategies

used in building meaning. What never ceases to amaze students is how the predominantly used strategy often differs from reader to reader. Sometimes I have students download their thinking through writing. They respond in journals, take notes, flag points for discussion with sticky notes, or complete graphic organizers; through each activity they're thinking in print. However, there's a caveat for these types of thinking tools.

First, I use thinking tools that align with worthwhile strategies; the tools help students work through the procedure of the strategy. Second, I've found that comprehension projects can't just be assigned, collected, and corrected. They won't teach students to comprehend. But the discussion around them will. Access tools (e.g., journals, note sheets, graphic organizers) can help students, but the students have to use them for thinking, not merely as writing activities. The content of the text and associated objectives dictate which strategies I plan and which thinking tools we use (Tovani 2000).

The next three sections succinctly identify the cognitive skills Irwin (1991) associates with the macro, elaborative, and metacognitive levels of comprehension. Glitches in these areas are ameliorated as students become proficient with the mind work associated with each area. Following those sections, I describe several procedures for specific comprehension strategies with step-by-step explanation. It's soon apparent that procedures for these strategies are multidimensional and include macro, elaborative, and/or metacognitive thinking, blurring the lines between thinking behaviors. Irwin (1991) intended the categories as a conceptual framework for understanding the components of comprehension, not as a one-way flowchart for thinking.

If . . . Then Scenarios for Problems at the Macro Level

The macro level deals with the big picture; students are discerning what the text was mostly about. They construct (mentally, verbally, or in writing) a gist statement or longer summary. If students can't retell what they read with a logical connection of ideas, I demonstrate the prerequisite thinking that's needed. I model, model, model verbally and in print how I construct a gist paragraph and summary. But I make sure to emphasize that mine isn't the only possible summary.

There isn't a single perfect summary for any text. I want students to determine the importance of particular ideas in the text (Zimmermann and Hutchins 2003), deciding which they'll focus on. It's easier for them to do that when they have a purpose for reading (Tovani 2000). My students also decide how to organize the important information (main ideas) and details they've gathered (Irwin 1991). What readers deem important and their summaries reflect the lives they bring to the text.

But I also want students to move beyond a summary. I encourage them to elaborate on the text—to fold into it what they know and have experienced. The result is a personal comprehension gumbo.

If . . . Then Scenarios for Problems at the Elaborative Level

My students' prior experiences and background knowledge influence the sophistication and amount of elaborating they do. In other words, what they bring thickens the gumbo. Elaborating or adding to the text involves both reading *between the lines* (inferring) and reading *beyond the lines* (synthesizing). When my students aren't making inferences or synthesizing with text, I show them what it looks like when someone does that kind of thinking in her daily life. Then, I repeatedly model the same thinking with texts we're using.

Tovani states that "inferring is abstract thinking" (2000, 101). It requires that we blend our life experiences and prior knowledge with the text on the page to construct understanding. My inference demonstration for students might sound like this.

T: When we checked in we handed our luggage to a bellhop who delivered it to our room. Where was I?

S: You were at a hotel.

T: I didn't say that. How did you know?

S: Cuz you said a bellhop.

T: Why couldn't I have been at a motel or a campground?

S: Cuz they're not fancy-smancy. There aren't bellhops at motels.

S2: Yeah, and motels aren't built high with lots of floors. They usually only have one or two floors and you carry everything yourself. Ugh!

S3: The bellhop puts your luggage on a rolling cart. Sometimes, if he has other people's luggage, he gets to your room after you've checked it out.

S4: Yeah, bellhops help you, but they expect a tip. You're supposed to give so much for every bag. That's what my dad said. Sometimes, my dad has us lug our own stuff.

T: How do you know all this about hotels?

S: I stayed at a hotel when we went to my cousin's wedding.

S3: Me too. I've been to one. Only, it was when we went on vacation.

S4: I haven't been to a bellhop place, but I saw a movie where it worked like that.

S2: I didn't see it in a movie or go there, but I heard about bellhops.

T: It sounds like you were mixing what you knew with what the author said. You made a logical leap. You mixed the information I gave you with your experiences or what you knew, and then you inferred I was in a hotel even though I never said that. Readers make inferences all the time. It's essential. You need to constantly be mixing what's in your head with what's in the text to—voila—draw an inference out of your mind. We make inferences all day long.

I tell students that they're inferring all the time during interactions with other people. I've noticed them respond to someone who looked sad. I've heard them ask, "What's the matter?" By noticing that person's expression and considering what it meant, they inferred that sympathetic listening was needed. "Inferring is the bedrock of comprehension, not only in reading. We infer in many realms" (Harvey and Goudvis 2000, 105).

I also point out to students that predicting is related to inferring. Recognizing the theme and the main idea also requires a degree of inferring. Some of the details they add when visualizing are inferred. In each case, they combine schemata and the text to make a logical leap—one that's original because the mix they bring to the text is unique (Harvey and Goudvis 2000). "Inferring occurs at the intersection of questioning, connecting, and print" (96). I want students to appreciate that inferring adds their voices to comprehension.

My students' voices involve the "reservoirs of [personal] experience, knowledge, and feeling" (Rosenblatt 1978), stirred by the author's words. In the process of talking, students teach each other about their lives. These reservoirs become the grist of critical discussions. When answering questions posed by peers, students begin to define their place in an issue. Conversation provides students a lens on different perspectives, allowing them to develop empathy and a respect for diverse ideas. However, questions and respectful challenges demand *grounding*—a rationale or defense for one's position (Calkins 2001). I want students to understand that although it's important to have informed opinions, people won't take you seriously unless your points are supported by facts or the text.

Students take a position after synthesizing what they've read and learned. They move beyond the lines in the text but remain influenced by the author's words. "Synthesizing text involves linking new information with prior knowledge or with multiple texts to develop a new idea, establish a new way of thinking, or create a new product of some type" (Tankersley 2005, 151). I've often used the following example to explain synthesizing to students.

> Imagine that you were studying problems associated with land pollution. You read many books, watched videos, heard speakers, and discussed the issue with others. After these experiences, you were asked to design a recycling plan for your community. That plan would be the result of your synthesis. You would use what you learned to create a new plan. It would be an original idea, but one influenced by what you had learned.

In such a creative process, students analyze information in a variety of ways, including categorizing, classifying, comparing, distinguishing, selecting, surveying, subdividing, and evaluating (Tankersley 2005). And all this thinking cannot happen in a vacuum. I tell students they need to be at the helm of their comprehension. They're in charge! They need to be aware of what's going on in their heads.

If . . . Then Scenarios for Problems at the Metacognitive Level

If students expect me to be the only one who assesses comprehension, they stop worrying about how well they understand what they're reading (Tovani 2000). And that's a big problem. Just as a person needs to be vigilantly aware of personal signs of health, readers need to regularly take their comprehension pulse. Early detection makes glitch recovery easier.

I want students to act metacognitively—always aware of their understanding. But when my students aren't doing that or can't do that, I have to show them what thinking about thinking looks like. That's another place where think-alouds help.

I verbalize self-questioning, predicting, and struggling with concepts, words, or the author's style of writing. I verbalize plans for solving each dilemma as it erupts. I show students how I put strategies into action—offensively and defensively. I work offensively when I apply the protocols of a particular strategy as I read. I act defensively when I immediately take out my toolbox of fix-up strategies to repair any glitches along the way. Efficient switching from offense to defense requires that I know when my reading is clicking along and when I'm in trouble.

I've found that struggling readers are oblivious to their disintegrating understanding. And when they do sense it, they don't know what to do. I understand their feelings of frustration. It's what I feel every time my computer meets a glitch. I want to know how to fix it myself instead of having to wait for help. To empower my students with repairman skills, we work on strategies that effectively integrate the macro, elaborative, and metacognitive levels of comprehension. And many of these strategies indirectly reinforce skills at the micro and integrative levels as well.

Just as any handyman needs the right tool to do a job well, readers need the strategy du jour—the one for that moment or the one that works on the glitch at hand. And they have to adeptly and independently know how to use that tool. So my instructional goal is two-pronged. I need to help students build their bank of known strategies—to know these in a cognitive or academic sense. But I also have to be sure that they are fully prepared to transfer this knowledge in the act of reading; proficient readers can select the most appropriate strategy tool and effortlessly repair the glitch *on the run*.

I've selected five strategies that are comprehensive, research-based, and have a track record of effectiveness. But, as previously mentioned, there are many others. There's considerable overlap with the components of effective strategies; they begin to look like a rose by another name. But their similar characteristics reflect central essential factors. Deep comprehension requires active mental and emotional engagement from the reader. It requires recursive thinking—verifying, substantiating, connecting, feeling, analyzing, evaluating, and on and on.

You'll notice that questioning and conversation are central to the strategies I emphasize. Gradually, my students can just as adeptly turn their questions and responses inward at will. At that point they've internalized self-talk and have begun to use it when reading independently. But my students still—as would be expected of literate people—enjoy (and benefit from) lively conversations with peers; they relish the talk that helps them *chew and digest* texts they've read.

Strategies for Deep Understanding

Reciprocal Teaching

Reciprocal teaching is a strategy that includes four steps in the process of building understanding with text (Palincsar and Brown 1984; Fisher and Frey 2004). The steps direct readers to predict, question, clarify, and summarize. Each step is grounded in current knowledge of best practices for comprehension instruction (Flood, Lapp, and Fisher 2003; Harvey and Goudvis 2000; Keene and Zimmermann 1997); each requires the reader to self-check for understanding.

I model the whole process multiple times, using texts related to current classroom studies. I intentionally demonstrate my back-and-forth cha-cha with the steps. I want students to see that the steps are not executed in a strict linear order. We discuss what they saw, what (particular steps) I was doing, and why.

One by one, I hand steps off to students, who contribute their part to a demonstration. Again we analyze the strategy demonstration in detail. Eventually, they complete all four steps and I facilitate the class debriefing. We talk about each step and how they interacted.

Prediction
We discuss

- what we predicted; what we wondered
- when we predicted; when our curiosity was aroused
- why we predicted
- what clues influenced our predictions; what made us curious
- whether the text followed our predictions

Question
We ask ourselves questions that

- check our recall of information
- call for inferences, linking the text with our experiences and prior knowledge
- lead to thinking beyond the text

Clarify
We explain and substantiate our responses and ask others to do the same in order to

- clear up confusions or fill in gaps
- give support for thinking
- determine when and how ideas need revision
- decide on strategies (plans) for resolving any dissonance in thinking

Summarize
We sum up, including essential vocabulary used by the author as we retell

- the theme and main ideas as we perceive them
- key concepts, people, places, or items described in the text

Reciprocal teaching fluidly and dynamically incorporates skills in the macro, elaborative, and metacognitive realms. The activity also generates supportive meaning building, helping all to see how thinking works. "Reciprocal teaching provides teachers with a planned way for students to assume responsibility for their learning and the learning of peers" (Fisher and Frey 2004, 167).

The next strategy is also based on reciprocity that's eventually internalized as independent self-questioning followed by self-responding.

ReQuest: Reciprocal Questioning

The questioning protocols of the ReQuest strategy direct students to

- form their own questions before, during, and after reading
- use self-questioning when setting purposes for reading
- read with an inquisitive stance
- develop a self-monitoring system (Manzo 1968)

It's quickly apparent why this procedure yields very different results each time it's used. It's amazing and wonderful! If transcripts of the discourse in two classrooms were examined, one might wonder how the same text could have been read in each. The spontaneity of students' personal wonderings initiates an exchange that flows in a manner similar to the following.

ReQuest Strategy

1. The teacher and students silently read a section of text.

2. The teacher puts the text aside. Students pose all types of questions to the teacher. The teacher answers each. Whenever a question is unclear, the teacher seeks clarification or elaboration from the asker. This improves students' ability to precisely express what they want to know.

3. The roles of asker and responder are reversed. Students put the text aside. The teacher asks all types of questions, modeling what to ask and how to word queries. Students can similarly seek clarification or elaboration from the teacher when a question is unclear. Students answer the teacher's questions, grounding their responses with support from the text, experiences, and background knowledge.

4. The teacher asks students to formulate logical predictions for what will come next in the reading.

5. If students' predictions are logical, the teacher directs them to read another section before cycling back to the first step in the strategy. If their predictions

are inappropriate, the teacher gives instruction in making supportable predictions and provides demonstrations.

6. When the complete text has been read, the class discusses it as a whole. The teacher invites students to share their comments and reactions.

In the ReQuest procedure, the questions asked determined the aspect—macro, elaborative, or metacognitive—of deeper comprehension that students are focusing on. The collaborative nature of the process allows dual control. Students explore their own wonderings; the teacher poses questions that direct students' thinking in specific channels. And because of this back-and-forth discussion, students appreciate the range of questions that are appropriate to ask, how answers are constructed for each type, and the personal nature of responses to deep questions.

The next strategy focuses on building personal meaning, bit by bit. This helps students who are mystified by how that process occurs.

GIST: Generating Interactions Between Schemata and Text

The GIST procedure begins with the integrative level, discussed in Chapter 9. It requires the reader to string meaning across sentences on the way to building an understanding of the text in larger units (paragraphs to subsections) and, then, as a whole (Cunningham 1982). The activity provides "a prescription for reading from group sentence-by-sentence gist production to individual whole paragraph gist production" (42).

I find that students who've had a chance to download their thinking and revise the gist they've created express their conclusions clearly and competently. Their talk becomes a tool for carving out the unnecessary and refining what's essential. When the sculpting is complete, students efficiently summarize what they understand.

The steps presented here are for a short passage.

GIST Strategy

1. The teacher selects a passage for reading. A somewhat easy passage with four or five paragraphs is best for introducing the strategy.

2. The teacher directs students to read the first paragraph and think how they'd retell the gist of what they've read in twenty (or fewer) words.

3. Students cover the paragraph and write their twenty-word (or fewer) gist summary. A review of the paragraph is allowed when needed, but students should

cover it again before they continue writing to ensure ideas they remember are rephrased. I have students share and compare their gist summaries.

4. Students read the second paragraph and think about how they'd retell the first two paragraphs in a twenty-word (or fewer) gist summary that integrated key ideas from both. Students write their twenty-word gist summary. Again, I have students share and compare gist summaries. Continue this procedure of combining paragraphs to the end of the passage.

5. After the last paragraph has been read, students think about, write, share, and compare their twenty-word (or fewer) personally constructed gist summaries for the passage as a whole.

This construction of summaries is like the recite step in the SQ3R strategy that follows because it involves self-recitation of key ideas and details from the text.

SQ3R: Survey, Question, Read, Recite, and Review

The SQ3R strategy is *tried and true*. It's been around and used widely for a long time because it's effective. The steps of Robinson's (1961) study method are basic, easy to remember, and, most importantly, grounded in sensible procedures for efficient learning with texts. There's a recursive nature to them. At any point, readers can go backward before moving forward to the next step.

SQ3R

1. *Survey*: Students look over the text (or passage) they'll be reading. They skim and scan, reading titles, subtitles, captions, pictures, charts, graphs, and any other visual or textual aids.

2. *Question*: Students pose questions that establish a purpose for reading. Predictions and wondering could also be included in this purpose-setting step. With steps 1 and 2, students are doing a walk and talk.

3. *Read*: Students read the text. Questions (or predictions) are revised and new ones added as the reader progresses through the text. Students should be self-monitoring for understanding and applying fix-up strategies when needed.

4. *Recite*: Students engage in self-talk or conversation with others to chew and digest what they recall and the meaning they've constructed with the text. A dialogue (with self or others) occurs segment by segment as the reader proceeds

through the text. Students reread whenever necessary to clarify confusions or to support conclusions.

5. *Review*: Students create their own closure as they sum up all that they've learned with the text, defining key concepts and integrating their interpretations, conclusions, and evaluations.

SQ3R is typically associated with content area reading because it's classified as a study strategy. However, it's equally effective with narrative text. Whether it's used with informational or narrative text, SQ3R integrates several strategies in a logical sequence—one that demands students' active engagement before, during, and after reading. The steps of this strategy appear to be a parent to the next strategy.

KWL: What Do You Know? What Do You Want to Know? What Did You Learn?

It would be difficult to find a teacher who hasn't heard of and used Ogle's (1986) KWL strategy. Even adaptations of this process are everywhere! Many of those adaptations are tailored to the specific needs of a topic. However, Atwell (1990) added another step—one that evokes metacognitive behavior. The reader asks himself, How will I find out? In the H phase students determine a plan for finding answers to their own questions. They decide specifically what they will do and what they will use. The modified strategy becomes KWHL.

KWL		
What Do You Know?	What Do You Want to Know?	What Did You Learn That You Didn't Already Know?
Students brainstorm all that they know or think they know on the topic. I (or they) write their statements in the K column. All statements are accepted as tentative. I ask students how they know what they know; I ask for evidence that supports each point. Statements are verified or corrected as we explore the text for answers.	Students pose questions or wonder statements that indicate what they expect to learn with this text. I always find that these extend beyond the initial text, sending students to others sources for answers.	Students recall what they've learned by recording it in the L column. They cross-check information they've learned with statements in the K column to verify or correct their initial brainstorming. I have students check off answered questions in the W column and determine what's left for further research.

The K column requires my students to do a mental survey of prior knowledge; they sort through ideas and bring what's relevant to the front burner in their mind. Our discussion of prior knowledge leads us to pose questions for the W column—questions that check, refine, and extend what we know. Our questions pique interest and create genuine purposes for reading. I find that students never fail to ask high-level questions that reach beyond the scope of the text at hand. My students' questions lead us into investigations with other sources. We also begin to code our statements in ways (e.g., footnotes) that indicate where we found answers, helping students realize the importance of citing sources. Throughout our collaborative KWHL work and students' self-talk, strategies for deep comprehension are naturally integrated, reinforced, and internalized.

Conclusion

An expression I heard long ago—so long ago that I don't remember its source—comes to mind when I think about strategy instruction. It explains why I emphasize it and schedule the time for guided practice in each strategy minilesson. That expression is "If you give a man a fish, you feed him for a day. If you teach him how to fish, you feed him for a lifetime." I want my students stocked up for a lifetime!

Effective strategies allow my students to navigate their mind journeys with increasing independence. In *Oh, the Places You'll Go*, Dr. Seuss tells readers that they are in charge. With brain power and effort as fuel, they can steer life's ship wherever they choose (Seuss 1990). I want students to experience their inner locus of control for success.

My instruction and group interactions provide *sustaining feedback*—feedback that shows them paths to follow as they construct and revise their own meaning. Sustaining feedback is inherently different from *corrective feedback* because it puts the student in control while guiding from the side. Corrective feedback is terminal; it simply identifies a student's error and supplies the correct (expected) response (Cole 2004). Anderson, Armbruster, and Roe (1990) found that although sustaining feedback is infrequently used, students' reading achievement is enhanced more with sustaining feedback than it is with corrective feedback.

The next chapter talks about successful implementation of strategy interventions, specifically finding the will, the time, and a way to do them.

11

Implementing Interventions

Finding Time

"You want me to do what? Where's the time for that with all we're supposed to teach now?" I hear this all the time; I feel it too. But I know deep down when we don't have the time it's usually because we don't have the will. We find time for what we value.

I want students to thrive in my classroom. If I don't do what I *really* need to do, many won't have an opportunity to learn. Simply covering curriculum by blazing over every mandate or standard doesn't amount to much. If my focus were coverage, I'd likely create *veneer learning* that looked good temporarily but quickly flaked off because it hasn't been rooted solidly in students' minds and hearts (Shea, Murray, and Harlin 2005).

We all have a given amount of time in the classroom; it's how we prioritize what we'll do with it that creates differences. I must choose to do more than simply cover material. I want to uncover students' inquiries and remove roadblocks so real learning can occur. Moving from curricular coverage to learning doesn't mean abandoning standards. A focus on standards is woven into my fabric of meaningful activities with relevant, interesting, and accessible informational resources. I'm continuously teaching to and assessing for acquisition of the standards. My assessment with MRRs is different; it's *portable* rather than anchored to a one-time or end-of-year measure. Portable assessments are particularly important for struggling readers.

Using Portable Assessments to Inform Instruction

Portable assessments are ones that can be used spontaneously. They're *formative* because they're less formal, allow the continuous assessment of development, and form the basis for instructional decision making (Lapp and Flood 2005).

It's like taking your pulse during exercise to determine how you should adjust the routine—slow down or pick up the pace. Portable assessments pinpoint glitches accurately and instantly, allowing them to be repaired before they escalate. MRRs are portable assessments because teachers

- use their own professional knowledge of the reading process and the MRR procedures to gather data and analyze students' performance
- use texts students are already reading in the classroom. Special material isn't needed
- use the results to make informed decisions about the next instructional step

Monitoring Throughout Lessons

As well as using the MRR procedure described in this text, listen to students retell and discuss material they've read on their own. Are they able to comfortably express the gist of what they read as well as add inferences, interpretations, conclusions, and evaluations? Based on the results of MRRs and classroom observations, do things differently. Differentiate the texts used in the classroom; differentiate the way they're used and the way students express their understanding. Full-time MRR thinking comes with practice; it's a journey.

Putting all this together can be overwhelming when tackling the job alone. But collaboration divides the burden and exponentially increases the number of ideas on the table. Students also sense the congruency of instruction and learning goals shared within the team of teachers and across our subject areas.

Working with Colleagues

When we share what we know about students and the instructional strategies we've tried, we increase the likelihood of success—for students and ourselves (Medway and Updike 1985). Friend and Cook define this collaboration in schools as "interaction between at least two co-equal parties voluntarily engaged in shared decision making as they work toward a common goal" (1990, 92).

My first rung of collaboration is my association with the grade-level team members. We meet regularly to discuss students' progress. In these exchanges we cover topics similar to the following.

- The difficulties associated with the range of learning levels in our classes.
- Which instructional strategies work best with whom and which don't. We brainstorm alternative directions instead of giving up on students.
- Particular dilemmas with individual students.
- Collective data for the grade or for the school as a whole. This helps us identify overall areas of strength and weakness (Cooper and Kiger 2005).
- How to recognize and avoid activities that *drill the skill and kill the will* to engage in mind journeys with texts.

Another level of collaboration involves the insights gained from conversations with building-level specialists and paraprofessionals who work with my students. These include special area teachers, special education teachers, remedial teachers, speech teachers, and ESL teachers, among others. I want to know how my students perform in these different settings, which frequently differ from my classroom in the teacher–student ratio, curriculum, and nature of activities. Additional details from these colleagues complete my portrait of each learner.

Collaboration with colleagues is a complex process. It operates with members as equals—no defined leaders and followers. When the interaction is open to diverse thinking, it improves my teaching; it also improves teaching across the school. "Collaboration works best when the adults involved bring their own unique strengths to the process" (Jaeger 1998, 93).

Publicly Celebrating Success and Nudging Forward

Mind journeys can be difficult and exhausting. Words of encouragement energize the traveler when persistence starts to fade. My students and I initially respond to each other's work with compliments. Students tell each other what they like, agree with, are intrigued by, and so on. Compliments act as a buffer for the comments that follow. Comments that nudge students toward deeper thinking and deeper expressing are respectfully offered. Comments tend to ask for more information, or clarification, or whether there's evidence for the expressed position.

Through compliments and comments, my students and I diagnostically respond to learning performances. The sharing encourages and nudges recipients forward to work on specific needs. I find that students more fully understand and appreciate the purpose of my assessments when they've experienced compliments and comments from each other.

Teaching Diagnostically, Teaching Differentially with Forward Vision

To teach diagnostically, I need to simultaneously wear two hats. One is the teaching hat and the other the assessing hat. Routman reports, "The most effective teachers constantly evaluate students' learning and needs *as* they are teaching" (2003, 205).

I act in different ways when wearing each hat and my results in one phase inform my actions in the other. Walker describes diagnostic teaching as "the process of using assessment and instruction at the same time to identify the instructional modifications that enable problem readers to become independent learners" (2004, 3).

In my back-and-forth dance with the learner, I lead off with a presentation of new material or skills. This is the teaching phase. Then I waltz with the learner as he practices the skill with text. All the while, I'm monitoring his footwork. I provide support in the form of prompts to determine if he knows the steps but feels hesitant about taking them. Or, is he using but confusing the application of the skill in this situation? Such assessing occurs in the diagnostic phase and tells me the next direction to take. Walker states, "the diagnostic teacher is an active problem-solver" (3). I focus, step by step, on responding to my partner—on working with him until he grasps the text—much like *feeling* the direction of steps in a dance. When I succeed at teaching diagnostically, the dance is graceful; the learner and I feel the energy of the art form.

This form of teaching allows me to respond immediately, nipping problems in the bud. It's so much easier to resolve tangles before they grow. It's something like *a stitch in time saves nine*. To successfully teach diagnostically, I need to know the reader as an individual and as a learner; I need to know the expectations for the reading process. I have to be an expert glitch detector who's able to efficiently apply what I learn diagnostically in the teaching phase, matching appropriate interventions to each glitch. And, finally, I need to dissolve glitches and put readers back on track each time without missing a step—or only a few! MRRs help me accomplish these goals.

Afterword

At first people refuse to believe that a strange new thing can be done, then they begin to hope it can be done, then they see it can be done—then it is done and all the world wonders why it was not done centuries ago

—Frances Burnett, *The Secret Garden*

What I've proposed in this text might seem like a strange new thing for middle school and some may refuse to believe that it's possible. But I know everyone would hope that it could be done because the reasons for doing it are sound and the benefits are enormous.

For me there's no assessment on this earth that gives as much genuine data on a reader's performance at a given moment than a running record. Running records allow me to instantly find out what I need to know about learners in a way that builds trust. "I've discovered that thinking together with the learner makes the analysis easier, the relationship stronger, and builds self-reflection skills that go far beyond literacy situations" (Shea 2000, 126).

I suspect that the process for MRR described in this text will spark systemic change in the way things are done in your classroom and in your school. When you begin to work with readers in this way, they will respond differently. You will too. It always works that way because the process makes teaching and learning more personal—more focused on the individual. "Each reader I work with enlightens me about the reading process, the way literacy skills are acquired and develop, the power of collaborative evaluation and goal setting, and the effectiveness of my teaching" (Shea 2000, 126).

As you reflect and process the concepts in this text, let the vision of an MRR model of assessing and teaching evolve—see it working. Then slowly try it out. Have patience with your own learning curve. Share your journey and others will follow. Then we'll all wonder why we didn't always believe in the possibility.

References

Afflerbach, P., and P. Johnston. 1986. "What Do Expert Readers Do When the Main Idea Is Not Explicit?" In *Teaching Main Idea Comprehension*, ed. J. F. Baumann, 49–72. Newark, DE: International Reading Association.

Allan, K., and M. Miller. 2000. *Literacy and Learning: Strategies for Middle and Secondary School Teachers*. New York: Houghton Mifflin.

Allen, J. 1999. *Words, Words, Words*. Portland, ME: Stenhouse.

Allington, R. 1983. "Fluency: The Neglected Reading Goal." *The Reading Teacher* 36: 555–61.

———. 2001. *What Really Matters for Struggling Readers*. New York: Longman.

Anderson, R., B. Armbruster, and M. Roe. 1990. "Improving the Education of Reading Teachers." *Daedelus* 119: 187–210.

Anderson, R., and P. D. Pearson. 1984. "A Schema-Theoretic View of Basic Processes in Reading Comprehension." In *Handbook of Reading Research*, ed. P. D. Pearson, 255–91. White Plains, NY: Longman.

Atwell, N. 1990. *Coming to Know*. Portsmouth, NH: Heinemann.

Bear, D., M. Invernizzi, S. Templeton, and F. Johnston. 2000. *Words Their Way: Word Study for Phonics, Vocabulary, and Spelling Instruction*. Upper Saddle River, NJ: Merrill Prentice Hall.

Beck, I., and M. McKeown. 1991. "The Conditions of Vocabulary Acquisitions." In *Handbook of Reading Research*, Vol. 2, ed. R. Barr, M. Kamil, P. Mosenthal, and P. D. Pearson, 789–814. White Plains, NY: Longman.

Beck, I., E. McCaslin, and M. McKeown. 1980. "The Rationale and Design of a Program to Teach Vocabulary to Fourth Grade Students." ERDC Publication 1980/25. Pittsburgh: Pittsburgh Learning Research and Development Center, Pittsburgh University.

Beck, I., M. McKeown, and E. McCaslin. 1980. "All Contexts Are Not Created Equal." *Elementary School Journal* 83: 177–81.

Benson, V., and C. Cummins. 2000. *The Power of Retelling: Developmental Steps for Building Comprehension.* Chicago: Wright Group/McGraw-Hill.

Blachowicz, C., and P. Fisher. 2000. "Vocabulary Instruction." In *Handbook of Reading Research,* vol. 3, ed. M. Kamil, P. Mosenthal, P. Pearson, and R. Barr, 503–23. Mahwah, NJ: Erlbaum.

Bower, G. 1978. "Experiments on Story Comprehension and Recall." *Discourse Processes* 1: 211–31.

Brown, A., J. Day, and E. Jones. 1983. "The Development of Plans for Summarizing Texts." *Child Development* 54: 968–79.

Brown, A., and A. Palincsar. 1985. *Reciprocal Teaching of Comprehension Strategies: A Natural History of One Program to Enhance Learning.* Tech. Rep. 334. Urbana, IL: University of Illinois Center for the Study of Reading.

Brown, H., and B. Cambourne. 1998. *Read and Retell: A Strategy for the Whole Language/ Natural Learning Classroom.* Portsmouth, NH: Heinemann.

Burnett, F. 1911. *The Secret Garden.* New York: HarperCollins.

Cannon, W. 1939. *The Wisdom of Body.* New York: W. W. Norton.

Calkins, L. 2001. *The Art of Teaching Reading.* New York: Longman.

Cecil, N., and J. Gipe. 2003. *Literacy in the Intermediate Grades.* Scottsdale, AZ: Holcomb Hathaway.

Chard, D., S. Vaughn, and B. Tyler. 2002. "A Synthesis of Research on Effective Interventions for Building Fluency with Elementary Students with Learning Disabilities." *Journal of Learning Disabilities* 35: 386–406.

Clay, M. 1991. *Becoming Literate: The Construction of Inner Control.* Portsmouth, NH: Heinemann.

———. 1993. *An Observational Survey of Early Literacy Achievement.* Portsmouth, NH: Heinemann.

———. 2000. *Running Records for Classroom Teachers.* Portsmouth, NH: Heinemann.

Cole, A. 2004. *When Reading Begins.* Portsmouth, NH: Heinemann.

Cooper, J. D., and N. Kiger. 2005. *Literacy Assessment: Helping Teachers Plan Instruction.* New York: Houghton Mifflin.

Cunningham, J. 1982. "Generating Interaction Between Schema and Text." In *New Inquiries in Reading Research and Instruction. Thirty-First Yearbook of the National Reading Conference*, ed. J. Niles and L. Harris, 42–47. Oak Creek, WI: National Reading Conference.

Davenport, M. R. 2002. *Miscues Not Mistakes: Reading Assessment in the Classroom.* Portsmouth, NH: Heinemann.

Delpit, L. 1991. "Skills and Other Dilemmas of a Progressive Black Educator." *Harvard Educational Review* 56 (4): 379–85.

Dickinson, D., and M. Smith. 1994. "Long-Term Effect of Preschool Teachers' Book Readings on Low-Income Children's Vocabulary and Story Comprehension." *Reading Research Quarterly* 29 (2): 105–21.

Dickinson, D., and P. Tabors. 2002. "Fostering Language and Literacy in Classrooms and Homes." *Young Children* 57 (2): 10–18.

Dixon-Kraus, L. 1996. *Vygotsky in the Classroom.* White Plains, NY: Longman.

Eisner, E. 1998. *The Kind of Schools We Need.* Portsmouth, NH: Heinemann.

Fader, D. 1976. *The New Hooked on Books.* New York: Berkley.

Fielding, L., and P. D. Pearson. 1994. "Reading Comprehension: What Works." *Educational Leadership* 52 (February): 62–68.

Fielding, L., P. Wilson, and R. Anderson. 1986. "A New Focus on Free Reading: The Role of Trade Books in Reading Instruction." In *The Context of School-Based Literacy,* ed. T. Raphael. New York: Random House.

Finders, M., and S. Hynds. 2003. *Literacy Lessons: Teaching and Learning with Middle School Students.* Upper Saddle River, NJ: Merrill Prentice Hall.

Fisher, D., and N. Frey. 2004. *Improving Adolescent Literacy: Strategies That Work.* Upper Saddle River, NJ: Pearson, Merrill Prentice Hall.

Flood, J., D. Lapp, and D. Fisher. 2003. "Reading Comprehension Instruction." In *Handbook of Research on Teaching the English Language Arts,* 2d ed., ed. J. Flood, D. Lapp, J. Jenson, and J. Squire, 931–41. Mahwah, NJ: Lawrence Erlbaum.

Flurkey, A. 1995. "Take Another Look at (Listen to) Shari." *Primary Voices K–6* 3 (4): 10–15.

———. 1998. "Reading as Flow: A Linguistic Alternative to Fluency." Occasional Paper 26, Program in Language and Literacy, College of Education, University of Arizona.

Fouche, R. 2005. "Lighting Made Easy." *Footsteps* 7 (1): 8–11.

Fountas, I., and G. Pinnell. 1996. *Guided Reading.* Portsmouth, NH: Heinemann.

———. 2001. *Guided Readers and Writers: Grades 3–6.* Portsmouth, NH: Heinemann.

Friedberg, B., and E. Strong. 1989. "Please Don't Stop There! The Power of Reading Aloud." In *Children's Literature in the Classroom: Weaving Charlotte's Web,* ed. J. Hickman and B. Cullinan, 39–48. Norwood, MA: Christopher-Gordon.

Friend, M., and L. Cook. 1990. "Collaboration as a Predictor of Success in School Reform." *Journal of Educational and Psychological Consultation* 1 (1): 69–86.

Garner, R. 1987. "Metacognition and Reading Comprehension." Cognition and Literacy Series (0893913987). Norwood, NJ: Ablex.

Goodman, K. 1973. "Psycholinguistic Universals in the Reading Process." In *Psycholinguistics and Reading,* ed. Frank Smith, 158–76. New York: Holt, Rinehart, and Winston.

———. 1976. "Miscue Analysis: Theory and Reality in Reading." In *Language and Literacy: The Selected Writings of Kenneth S. Goodman,* ed. F. Gollasch, 103–13. Boston: Routledge/Kegan Paul.

———. 1982. "Miscues: Windows on the Reading Process." In *Language and Literacy: The Selected Writings of Kenneth S. Goodman,* edited by F. Gollasch, 93–101. Boston: Routledge/Kegan Paul.

———. 1986. *What's Whole in Whole Language?* Portsmouth, NH: Heinemann.

Goodman, Y., and C. Burke. 1972. *Reading Miscue Inventory: Procedures for Diagnosis and Evaluation.* New York: Macmillan.

Goodman, Y., and A. Marek. 1996. *Retrospective Miscue Analysis.* Katonah, NY: Richard C. Owen.

Goodman, Y., D. Watson, and C. Burke. 1987. *Reading Miscue Inventory: Alternative Procedures.* Katonah, NY: Richard C. Owen.

Greaney, V., and M. Hegarty. 1987. "Correlates of Leisure-Time Reading." *Journal of Research in Reading* 10 (1): 3–20.

Harris, A., and E. Sipay. 1990. *How to Increase Reading Ability.* New York: Longman.

Harvey, S., and A. Goudvis. 2000. *Strategies That Work.* York, ME: Stenhouse.

Herrold, W. G. Jr., J. Stanchfield, and A. Serabian. 1989. "Comparisons of the Effect of a Middle School Literature-Based Listening Program on Male and Female Attitudes Toward Reading." *Educational Research Quarterly* 13 (4): 43–46.

Hilliard, A. 1989. *Testing and Tracking.* Video. Available from the National Association for the Education of Young Children, 1509 Sixteenth Street, NW, Washington, DC, 20036.

Holdaway, D. 1979. *The Foundations of Literacy.* Portsmouth, NH: Heinemann.

Hudson, R., H. Lane, and P. Pullen. 2005. "Reading Fluency Assessment and Instruction: What, Why, and How?" *The Reading Teacher* 58 (8): 702–14.

Indiana Department of Education. 2005. "Academic Standards and Resources: Fluency Rubric." Retrieved June 14, 2005, from www.indianastandardsresource.org/documents/1.pdf.

IRA (International Reading Association) Board of Directors. 2000. "Teaching All Children to Read: The Roles of the Reading Specialist: A Position Statement of the International Reading Association." *The Reading Teacher* 54: 115–19.

Irwin, J. 1991. *Teaching Reading Comprehension Processes*. 2d ed. Englewood Cliffs, NJ: Prentice Hall.

Jaeger, E. 1998. "The Reading Specialist as Collaborative Consultant." In *Teaching Struggling Readers*, ed. R. Allington, 91–99. Newark, DE: International Reading Association.

Johns, J. 1997. *Basic Reading Inventory*. Dubuque, IA: Kendall/Hunt.

Johnston, P. 1983. *Reading Comprehension Assessment: A Cognitive Basis*. Newark, DE: International Reading Association.

———. 1992. *Constructive Evaluation of Literate Activities*. Portsmouth, NH: Heinemann.

Just, M., and P. Carpenter. 1984. *The Psychology of Language and Reading Comprehension*. Boston: Allyn and Bacon.

Keene, E., and S. Zimmermann. 1997. *Mosaic of Thought: Teaching Comprehension in a Reader's Workshop*. Portsmouth, NH: Heinemann.

Ketch, A. 2005. "Conversation: The Comprehension Connection." *The Reading Teacher* 59 (1): 8–13.

Kibby, M. 2004. "Research-Based Strategies for Teaching Meaning Vocabulary." Presentation for the Graduate School Continuing Professional Education Series, Buffalo, NY, March 18.

Klinger, J., and S. Vaughn. 1999. "Promoting Reading Comprehension and English Acquisition Through Collaborative Strategic Reading." *The Reading Teacher* 52: 738–47.

Koskinen, P., L. Gambrell, B. Kapinus, and B. Heathington. 1988. "Retelling: A Strategy for Enhancing Students' Reading Comprehension." *The Reading Teacher* 41: 892–96.

Kugler, R. A. 2005. "Our Dependence on Oil." *Faces* 21 (6): 8–12.

Kuhn, M., and S. Stahl. 2000. *Fluency: A Review of Developmental and Remedial Practices*. CIERA Rep. 2-008. Ann Arbor, MI: Center for the Improvement of Early Reading Achievement.

Lamott, A. 1994. *Bird by Bird*. New York: Anchor.

Lapp, D., and J. Flood. 2005. "Understanding the Learner: Using Portable Assessment." In *After Early Intervention, Then What?* ed. R. McCormack and J. Paratore,

10–24. Newark, DE, and Upper Saddle River, NJ: International Reading Association and Pearson, Merrill Prentice Hall.

Leslie, L., and J. Caldwell. 2001. *Qualitative Reading Inventory*. New York: Allyn and Bacon.

Lowry, L. 1989. *Number the Stars*. New York: Bantam Doubleday Dell.

Manzo, A. 1968. "Improving Reading Comprehension Through Reciprocal Questioning." Doctoral diss., primary reference, Syracuse University, Syracuse, NY.

Manzo, A., U. Manzo, and M. Thomas. 2005. *Content Area Literacy*. Hoboken, NJ: John Wiley and Sons.

Medway, F., and J. Updike. 1985. "Meta-analysis of Consultation Outcome Studies." *American Journal of Community Psychology* 13: 489–505.

Moore, D., T. Bear, D. Birdyshaw, and J. Rycik. 1999. "International Reading Association's Position Statement on Adolescent Literacy." Retrieved December 21, 2004, from http://reading.org/resources/issues/positions_adolescent.html.

Nagy, W. 2004. *Teaching Vocabulary to Improve Reading Comprehension*. Newark, DE: International Reading Association.

Nagy, W., R. Anderson, and P. Herman. 1987. "Learning Word Meanings from Context During Normal Reading." *American Educational Research Journal* 24: 237–70.

Nagy, W., P. Herman, and R. Anderson. 1985. "Learning Words from Context." *Reading Research Quarterly* 20: 172–93.

Nagy, W., and J. A. Scott. 2000. "Vocabulary Processes." In *Handbook of Reading Research*, vol. 3, ed. M. Kamil, P. Mosenthal, P. Pearson, and R. Barr, 269–84. Mahwah, NJ: Lawrence Erlbaum.

New York State Education Department (NYSED). 2004. *Individual Evaluation Requirements for Specialists in Middle Childhood Education (Grades 5–9) and Adolescence Education (Grades 7–12)*. Retrieved December 21, 2004, from www.highered.nysed.gov/tcert/certificate/req-spec.htm.

Ogle, D. 1986. "K-W-L: A Teaching Model That Develops Active Reading of Expository Text." *The Reading Teacher* 39: 564–70.

Palincsar, A., and A. Brown. 1984. "Reciprocal Teaching of Comprehension-Fostering and Comprehension-Monitoring Activities." *Cognition and Instruction* 1: 117–75.

Pearson, P. D., L. Roehler, J. Dole, and G. Duffy. 1992. "Developing Expertise in Reading Comprehension." In *What Research Has to Say About Reading Instruction*, ed. J. Samuels and A. Farstrup, 145–99. Newark, DE: International Reading Association.

Perich, S. T. 2004. "Frith's Fabulous Photography." *Dig* 6 (4): 26.

Phinney, M. 1988. *Reading with the Troubled Reader*. Portsmouth, NH: Heinemann.

Pinnell, G. S., J. Pikulski, K. Wixon, J. Cambell, P. Gough, and A. Beatty. 1995. *Listening to Children Read Aloud: Oral Fluency*. Washington, DC: National Center for Education Statistics, U.S. Department of Education. Retrieved July 14, 2005, from http://nces.ed.gov/pubs/web/95762.asp.

Pikulski, J., and D. Chard. 2005. "Fluency: Bridge Between Decoding and Reading Comprehension." *The Reading Teacher* 58 (6): 510–19.

Pogrow, S. 2005. "HOTS Revisited: A Thinking Development Approach to Reducing the Learning Gap After Grade 3." *Phi Delta Kappan* 87 (1): 64–75.

Prescott-Griffin, M., and N. Witherell. 2004. *Fluency in Focus: Comprehension Strategies for All Young Readers*. Portsmouth, NH: Heinemann.

Rasinski, T. 2000. "Speed Does Matter in Reading." *The Reading Teacher* 54 (2): 146–51.

———. 2003. *The Fluent Reader*. New York: Scholastic.

———. 2005. "Assessing Reading Fluency." *Pacific Resources for Education and Learning*. Product ES0414. Retrieved June 8, 2005, from www.prel.org/oproducts/re_/assessing-fluency.htm.

Rasinski, T., and N. Padak. 1998. "How Elementary Students Referred for Compensatory Reading Instruction Perform on School-Based Measures of Word Recognition, Fluency, and Comprehension." *Reading Psychology: An International Quarterly* 19: 185–216.

Rasinski, T., N. Padak, C. McKeon, L. Wilfong, J. Friedauer, and P. Heim. 2005. "Is Reading Fluency a Key for Successful High School Reading?" *Journal of Adolescent and Adult Literacy* 49 (1): 22–27.

Robb, L. 2000. *Teaching Reading in Middle School*. New York: Scholastic.

Robinson, F. 1961. *Effective Study*. Rev. ed. New York: Harper and Row.

Roe, B., B. Stoodt-Hill, and P. Burns. 2004. *Secondary School Literacy Instruction: The Content Areas*. New York: Houghton Mifflin.

Rosenblatt, L. 1978. *The Reader, the Text, the Poem: The Transactional Theory of the Literature Work*. Carbondale: Southern Illinois University Press.

Routman, R. 2000. *Conversations: Strategies for Teaching, Learning and Evaluating*. Portsmouth, NH: Heinemann.

———. 2003. *Reading Essentials*. Portsmouth, NH: Heinemann.

Royer, J., and D. Cunningham. 1978. *On the Theory and Measurement of Reading Comprehension*. Tech. Rep. 91. ED 157 040. Urbana: Center for the Study of Reading, University of Illinois.

Rycik, J., and J. Irvin. 2005. *Teaching Reading in the Middle Grades*. New York: Pearson/ Allyn and Bacon.

Samuels, S. 2002. "Reading Fluency: It's Development and Assessment." In *What Research Has to Say About Reading Instruction*, 3d ed., ed. A. E. Farstrap and S. J. Samuels, 166–83. Newark, DE: International Reading Association.

Schreiber, P. 1980. "On the Acquisition of Fluency." *Journal of Reading Behavior* 12 (3): 177–86.

Schumm, J., S. Vaughn, and A. Leavell. 1994. "Planning Pyramid: A Framework for Planning for Diverse Student Needs During Content Area Instruction." *The Reading Teacher* 47: 608–15.

Seuss, Dr. 1978. *I Can Read with My Eyes Shut*. New York: Random House.

———. 1990. *Oh, the Places You'll Go*. New York: Random House.

Shea, M. 2000. *Taking Running Records*. New York: Scholastic.

———. 2004. "Teachers Guide for *I Didn't Know That!*" Retrieved February 10, 2004, from www.cobblestonepub.com/pages/nonfictionguideDidn'tKnow.html.

Shea, M., R. Murray, and R. Harlin. 2005. *Drowning in Data? How to Collect, Organize, and Document Student Performance*. Portsmouth, NH: Heinemann.

Smith, F. 1976. *Comprehension and Learning*. New York: Richard C. Owen.

———. 1977. "Making Sense of Reading—and Reading Comprehension." *Harvard Educational Review* 47: 386–95.

———. 1985. *Reading Without Nonsense*. New York: Teachers College Press.

Snow, C. 1993. "Families as Social Contexts for Literacy Development." In *The Development of Literacy Through Social Interaction*, ed. C. Daiute, 11–23. Cambridge, MA: Blackwell.

Stahl, S., and M. Fairbanks. 1986. "The Effects of Vocabulary Instruction: A Model-Based Meta-analysis." *Review of Educational Research* 56: 72–110.

Stahl, S., M. Richek, and R. Vandevier. 1991. "Learning Word Meanings Through Listening: A Sixth-Grade Replication." In *Learning Factors/Teacher Factors: Issues in Literacy Research. Fortieth Yearbook of the National Reading Conference*, ed. J. Zutell and S. McCormick, 185–92. Chicago: National Reading Conference.

Stecker, S., N. Roser, and M. Martinez. 1998. "Understanding Oral Reading Fluency." In *Forty-seventh Yearbook of the National Reading Conference*, ed. T. Shanahan and F. V. Rodriguez-Brown, 295–310. Chicago: National Reading Conference.

Tankersley, K. 2005. *Literacy Strategies for Grades 4–12*. Alexandria, VA: Association for Supervision and Curriculum Development.

Temple, C., D. Ogle, A. Crawford, and P. Freppon. 2005. *All Children Read: Teaching for Literacy in Today's Diverse Classrooms*. New York: Pearson/Allyn and Bacon.

Tierney, R., J. Readence, and E. Dishner. 1995. *Reading Strategies and Practices: A Compendium*. Boston: Allyn and Bacon.

Tomlinson, C. 2001. *How to Differentiate Instruction in Mixed-Ability Classrooms*. 2d ed. Alexandria, VA: Association for Supervision and Curriculum Development.

Tompkins, G. 2001. *Guidelines for Reading Comprehension Instruction*. Video. Upper Saddle River, NJ: Merrill Prentice Hall.

———. 2003. *Literacy for the 21st Century*. 3d ed. Upper Saddle River, NJ: Merrill Prentice Hall.

———. 2004. *Literacy for the 21st Century: Teaching Reading and Writing in Grades 4 Through 8*. Upper Saddle River, NJ: Pearson, Merrill Prentice Hall.

Tovani, C. 2000. *I Read It, But I Don't Get It*. Portland, ME: Stenhouse.

Urbanus, J. 2005. "Rebirth of a City." *Dig* 7 (3): 14–15.

Vacca, J., R. Vacca, M. Gove, L. Burkey, L. Lenhart, and C. McKeon. 2003. *Reading and Learning to Read*. 5th ed. New York: Allyn and Bacon.

van Dijk, T., and W. Kintsch. 1983. *Strategies for Discourse Comprehension*. New York: Academic.

Vygotsky, L. 1978. *Mind and Society: The Development of Higher Psychological Processes*. Cambridge: Harvard University Press.

Walker, B. 2004. *Diagnostic Teaching of Reading: Techniques for Instruction and Assessment*. Upper Saddle River, NJ: Pearson, Merrill Prentice Hall.

Wilhelm, J. 2001. *Improving Comprehension with Think-Aloud Strategies*. New York: Scholastic.

Wood, K. D. 1987. "Fostering Cooperative Learning in Middle and Secondary Classrooms." *Journal of Reading* 31: 10–18.

Yatvin, J. 2004. *A Room with a Differentiated View*. Portsmouth, NH: Heinemann.

Zimmermann, S., and C. Hutchins. 2003. *Seven Keys to Comprehension*. New York: Three Rivers.

Index